Divorcing a Narcissist

Prepare For a High-Conflict Divorce, Succeed in Family Court, Recover from Emotional Abuse, and Embrace a New Beginning Without Your Toxic Ex

Claire Brown

Copyright © 2024 Claire Brown. All rights reserved.

The content of this book may not be reproduced, duplicated, or transmitted without direct written permission from the author or the publisher.

Under no circumstances will any blame or legal responsibility be held against the publisher or author for any damages, reparation, or monetary loss due to the information contained within this book. Either directly or indirectly. You are responsible for your own choices, actions, and results. This is not legal advice.

Legal Notice: This book is copyright-protected. This book is only for personal use. You cannot amend, distribute, sell, use, quote, or paraphrase any part or the content within this book without the author's or publisher's consent.

Disclaimer Notice:

Please note the information contained within this document is for educational and entertainment purposes only. There is no legal advice being given. All effort has been executed to present accurate, up-to-date, and reliable, complete information. No warranties of any kind are declared or implied. Readers acknowledge that the author is not engaging in the rendering of legal, financial, medical, or professional advice. The content within this book has been derived from various sources. Please consult a licensed professional before attempting any techniques outlined in this book.

By reading this document, the reader agrees that the author is under no circumstances responsible for any losses and/or damages, direct or indirect, incurred as a result of using the information contained within this document, including, but not limited to, errors, omissions, or inaccuracies.

Contents

Introduction	1
1. Understanding Narcissistic Personality Disorder (NPD)	4
2. Preparing for the Legal Battle	17
3. Creating a Safety Plan	31
4. Financial Independence and Recovery	43
5. Emotional Healing and Self-Care	56
6. Co-Parenting with a Narcissist	67
7. Rebuilding Your Support Network	80
8. Navigating the Court System	91
9. Handling Narcissistic Retaliation	103
10. Overcoming Obstacles and Challenges	115
11. Embracing a New Beginning	125
Conclusion	137
References	140

Introduction

Sarah sat in her lawyer's office, feeling a mix of fear and relief. She had finally decided to divorce her husband, a man who had made her life a living nightmare. For years, she had endured emotional abuse, manipulation, and countless attempts to undermine her self-worth. Her husband was a classic narcissist—charming and charismatic to the outside world but cruel and controlling at home. As Sarah prepared for the legal battle ahead, she realized she was entering a new phase of her life, one fraught with challenges but also with the promise of freedom.

I wrote this book to be your guide through the intricate and often turbulent maze of divorcing a narcissist. It will prepare you emotionally and legally for what lies ahead. You will learn how to navigate the high-conflict divorce process, protect yourself and your children, and eventually rebuild your life. This book is here to empower you, to give you the tools and knowledge you need to succeed in family court, and to help you recover from the emotional abuse you have endured.

I am passionate about this topic because I have seen firsthand the devastating impact of narcissistic abuse. My name is Claire Brown, and I have lived through and survived this situation myself and helped others overcome these challenges. Through years of experience, research, counseling, and advocacy, I have gained a deep understanding of the complexities involved in divorcing a narcissist. I want to share this knowledge with you, offering you a roadmap to guide you through this difficult time.

Narcissistic Personality Disorder (NPD) is characterized by a pervasive pattern of grandiosity, a constant need for admiration, and a lack of empathy. People with NPD often display traits such as arrogance, a sense of entitlement, and a tendency to exploit others for personal gain. These traits make relationships with narcissists particularly challenging, as they are often manipulative, deceitful, and emotionally abusive. Understanding these traits is crucial as you prepare for the legal and emotional battles ahead.

When divorcing a narcissist, you will face specific legal challenges. Custody battles can become fierce, as narcissists often use children as pawns to control and manipulate you. Financial manipulation is another common tactic, with narcissists hiding assets or refusing to pay child support. In the courtroom, they may present themselves as the perfect parent or spouse, making it difficult for others to see their true nature. Knowing these strategies can help you prepare and protect yourself.

Emotionally, divorcing a narcissist can be a roller coaster. You may experience manipulation, gaslighting, and ongoing trauma. Narcissists are skilled at making you doubt your own reality, causing you to question your feelings and experiences. Understanding these tactics can help you recognize them for what they are and develop strategies to counteract them. This book's real-life examples and hypothetical scenarios will illustrate these points, helping you better understand and navigate your situation.

This book is structured to guide you step-by-step through the process. Each chapter will cover critical topics and provide actionable advice. Chapter 1 will delve into understanding narcissistic behavior and its impact on relationships. Chapter 2 will focus on preparing for the legal battle, including choosing the right lawyer and gathering evidence. Chapter 3 will discuss a safety plan. Chapter 4 will address financial challenges. Chapter 5 will offer strategies for emotional recovery and rebuilding your life. Chapter 6 discusses the importance of putting your children first and co-parenting with a narcissist. Chapter 7 will focus on rebuilding your support network. Chapter 8 will introduce you to the workings of the court system. Chapter 9 will prepare you for narcissistic retaliation. Chapter 10 will set your expectations for future obstacles and hurdles. Chapter 11 will show you how to start fresh and shed the baggage from your toxic relationship.

As you read this book, I encourage you to engage with the material, take notes, and apply the strategies discussed. Being proactive is key to navigating this journey successfully. Seek support from friends, family, and professionals. Remember, you are not alone in this process. Many have walked this path before you and have come out stronger on the other side.

Your experiences and feelings are valid. Divorcing a narcissist is one of the most challenging things you can go through, but it is also an opportunity for a new beginning. You have the strength and resilience to overcome this. This book will give you the knowledge, tactics, and confidence necessary to navigate this journey effectively.

So take a deep breath and know you are taking a courageous step towards a better future. This book is here to guide you, to support you, and to empower you. Together, we will navigate the legal and emotional challenges, and you will emerge stronger, wiser, and ready to embrace a new chapter in your life.

Chapter One

Understanding Narcissistic Personality Disorder (NPD)

When Emily first met Mark, she thought she had found her soulmate. He was charming, attentive, and seemed genuinely interested in her well-being. But as the months passed, subtle changes started to occur. Mark began criticizing her choices, belittling her accomplishments, and isolating her from friends and family. Emily felt increasingly confused and doubted her own perceptions. It wasn't until she stumbled upon an article about Narcissistic Personality Disorder (NPD) that she realized she was living with a narcissist. Understanding NPD was the first step in reclaiming her life.

This chapter aims to help you recognize and understand the traits of NPD, providing a foundation for the rest of the book. We will explore the diagnostic criteria, common misconceptions, and the specific characteristics that define narcissism. By the end of this chapter, you will have a clearer understanding of the behaviors you are dealing with and how they impact your relationship.

Identifying Narcissistic Traits

Narcissistic Personality Disorder (NPD) is a mental health condition characterized by a persistent pattern of grandiosity, a need for admiration, and a lack of empathy. According to the Diagnostic and Statistical Manual of Mental Disorders, Fifth Edition (DSM-5), NPD includes several diagnostic criteria. These criteria help clinicians identify and differentiate the disorder from other personality disorders. The DSM-5 outlines nine specific criteria, and an individual must exhibit at least five to be diagnosed with NPD. These criteria include a grandiose sense of self-importance, preoccupation with fantasies of unlimited success, a belief that they are "special" and unique, a need for excessive admiration, a sense of entitlement, exploitative behaviors, a lack of empathy, envy of others, and arrogant behaviors or attitudes.

A common misconception about narcissism is that it involves only self-love. In reality, narcissists often have a fragile self-esteem and use their grandiosity to mask deep insecurities. They seek validation from others to maintain their self-image, and any threat to this image can lead to aggressive or manipulative behaviors. Understanding these nuances is crucial in recognizing the true nature of NPD.

Narcissistic traits manifest in various ways. Grandiosity and self-importance are hallmark traits. A narcissist may exaggerate achievements, expect to be recognized as superior without commensurate accomplishments, and believe they deserve special treatment. For example, they might boast about their professional successes and demand admiration from colleagues and family members, even if their accomplishments are exaggerated or fabricated.

Lack of empathy is another defining trait. Narcissists struggle to recognize or care about the feelings and needs of others. This can lead to selfish behaviors and a disregard for the well-being of those around them. For instance, your partner might dismiss your feelings during an argument, showing little concern for your emotional state.

The need for excessive admiration is also prevalent. Narcissists crave constant validation and praise. They may seek out compliments and become angry or withdrawn if they feel neglected. This need for admiration can be exhausting for their partners, who often feel pressured to boost the narcissist's ego continuously.

A sense of entitlement is another common trait. Narcissists believe they deserve special treatment and privileges. They may expect others to cater to their needs without reciprocating. This sense of entitlement often leads to exploitative behaviors, where the narcissist uses others to achieve their own goals without considering the impact on those around them.

In relationships, these traits can create a toxic dynamic. Emotional manipulation is a frequent tactic. Narcissists may use guilt, shame, or fear to control their partners. They might twist facts, deny past statements, or shift blame to avoid taking responsibility. This manipulation can leave you feeling confused, anxious, and constantly on edge.

Patterns of control and dominance are also common. Narcissists seek to maintain power in the relationship, often by undermining your self-esteem and independence. They may isolate you from friends and family, criticize your choices, and make you feel incapable of making decisions without their input. This control can be subtle, gradually eroding your sense of autonomy.

Narcissism exists on a spectrum. Some individuals may exhibit mild narcissistic traits, while others display more severe behaviors. Overt narcissists are openly grandiose and seek attention through obvious means. They are often easy to identify due to their blatant arrogance and need for admiration. Covert narcissists, on the other hand, are more subtle. They may appear humble or self-effacing but still harbor a strong sense of entitlement and lack of empathy. Their manipulation is often more insidious and harder to detect.

Understanding the spectrum of narcissism helps you recognize that not all narcissists are the same. The intensity and manifestation of their traits can vary, influencing how they behave in relationships. Recognizing these differences is essential in developing effective strategies to protect yourself and navigate the challenges of divorcing a narcissist.

Understanding Gaslighting and Its Effects

Gaslighting is a particularly insidious form of psychological manipulation where the abuser seeks to make their victim doubt their own reality. The term "gaslighting" originated from the 1944 film *Gaslight*, in which a husband manipulates his wife into believing she is losing her sanity by subtly altering their environment and insisting she is mistaken or delusional when she notices the changes. This form of abuse creates a power dynamic that allows the manipulator to control the victim's perceptions, emotions, and actions.

Gaslighting techniques are varied but share a common goal: undermining the victim's sense of reality. One common tactic is denial and contradiction. The narcissist will blatantly deny having said or done something that the victim clearly remembers. For instance, you might recall a conversation where your partner promised to do something, but later, they vehemently denied ever making that promise. This constant denial can make you question your memory and sanity.

Another gaslighting tactic is trivializing the victim's feelings. The narcissist might dismiss your emotions as overly sensitive or irrational. When you express hurt or anger, they might say, "You're just being too sensitive" or "You're overreacting." This minimizes your feelings and makes you doubt their validity. Over time, you might start to suppress your emotions, believing that they are indeed exaggerated.

Blame-shifting and deflection are also common. The narcissist will often turn the tables during arguments, making you feel responsible for their abusive behavior. If you confront them about a hurtful comment, they might respond with, "If you weren't so difficult, I wouldn't have to say things like that." This deflection makes you feel guilty and responsible for the conflict, diverting attention from their actions.

The effects of gaslighting are profound and can be both immediate and long-lasting. In the short term, victims often experience a significant erosion of self-trust and confidence. They start to second-guess their memories and perceptions, leading to a state of constant confusion and self-doubt. This can make it challenging to make decisions or trust one's own judgment.

Over time, the cumulative effects of gaslighting can lead to severe psychological issues such as anxiety and depression. Constantly questioning one's reality and feeling invalidated can create a persistent sense of unease and hopelessness. Victims may isolate themselves from friends and family, believing that they are indeed "crazy" or unworthy of love and support.

Cognitive dissonance, a state of mental discomfort caused by holding contradictory beliefs, is another common effect. Victims of gaslighting struggle to reconcile their understanding of reality with the distorted version presented by the narcissist. This cognitive dissonance can be mentally exhausting and emotionally draining, making it difficult to break free from the abusive relationship.

Emily's experience with gaslighting began subtly. Her partner would frequently deny saying things that she vividly remembered. He would accuse her of imagining things or being forgetful when she confronted him. Over time, Emily started believing that she was losing her memory. She began to write down conversations and events to keep track of what actually happened, but even then, her partner would accuse her of fabricating the notes. This constant manipulation eroded Emily's self-confidence, making her feel isolated and dependent on her partner's version of reality.

Another example is John, whose partner trivializes his achievements and feelings. Whenever John shared his successes at work, his partner would downplay them, saying, "That's no big deal; anyone could do that." When he expressed his feelings of hurt or frustration, she would dismiss them with, "You're just being dramatic." Over time, John stopped sharing his accomplishments and emotions, believing they were indeed insignificant and unworthy of attention.

Gaslighting is a powerful tool of control that can leave deep psychological scars. Recognizing these tactics is the first step towards reclaiming your sense of reality and self-worth. By understanding the mechanisms of gaslighting, you can start to see through the manipulation and take steps to protect yourself.

Love Bombing and Future Faking Explained

Love bombing is a tactic that narcissists use to overwhelm their victims with excessive attention and affection. This method creates a powerful emotional bond, making it difficult for the victim to see the narcissist's true nature. The narcissist showers their partner with compliments, gifts, and grand gestures, making them feel special and adored. Suddenly, the narcissist seems like the perfect partner, attentive to every need and desire. This intense focus can be intoxicating, pulling the victim into a whirlwind romance that feels almost too good to be true.

The initial charm and idealization phase is the first stage of love bombing. During this period, the narcissist will go to great lengths to make their partner feel like the center of their universe. They may plan elaborate dates, send constant messages of love and admiration, and even make grand promises about the future. This stage creates a deep emotional connection, making the victim feel valued and cherished. However, this idealization is not based on genuine affection but rather on the narcissist's need to secure their control over the victim.

As the relationship progresses, the demands and expectations gradually increase. The narcissist begins to test the boundaries of their partner's devotion. Subtle requests for favors or sacrifices become more frequent, and the victim feels compelled to comply to maintain the affection they have grown accustomed to. The narcissist may start to isolate the victim from friends and family, insisting that they spend all their time together. This isolation further deepens the victim's dependency on the narcissist, making it harder for them to recognize the manipulation at play.

Future faking is another manipulation tactic often used alongside love bombing. This involves making grand promises about the future to keep the victim invested in the relationship. The narcissist might talk about marriage, children, or other long-term plans, creating a vision of a perfect future that keeps the victim hopeful and committed. These promises are rarely fulfilled, as they are designed to string the victim along, maintaining their emotional investment without any real intention of following through.

For example, a narcissist might promise a future filled with travel and adventure, painting a picture of an exciting life together. They might talk about buying a house or starting a family, making the victim feel secure and hopeful about their shared future. However, as time passes, these promises remain unfulfilled, and the narcissist always finds excuses for why the plans can't materialize yet. This tactic keeps the victim waiting and hoping, allowing the narcissist to maintain control without delivering on their promises.

Consider the case of Jessica, who met her narcissistic partner during a business trip. He was charming and attentive, making her feel special from the moment they met. Within weeks, he was talking about marriage and children, making grand declarations of love and commitment. Jessica felt like she had found her soulmate and eagerly invested in their future together. However, as months turned into years, those promises remained unfulfilled. Every time Jessica brought up their plans, her partner had an excuse or a reason to delay. The intense affection that had once been constant began to wane, replaced by periods of withdrawal and criticism. Jessica found herself trapped in a cycle of hope and disappointment, unable to break free from her partner's emotional hold over her.

Love bombing and future faking are powerful manipulation tools that create a deep sense of attachment and dependency. By recognizing these tactics, you can begin to see through the facade and understand the true nature of the relationship. Awareness is the first step towards breaking free and reclaiming your sense of self.

The Cycle of Narcissistic Abuse

The cycle of narcissistic abuse typically follows three distinct stages: idealization, devaluation, and discard. Each phase is unique in its impact on the victim, designed to create a complex web of emotional dependency and confusion. Understanding this cycle is crucial for recognizing the patterns of abuse and taking steps to protect oneself.

In the idealization phase, the narcissist puts their partner on a pedestal. They shower them with excessive flattery, attention, and affection, making the partner feel like the most important person in the world. This stage is intoxicating, filled with grand gestures, love letters, and endless praise. The narcissist might tell their partner they are their soulmate, making promises of a perfect future together. This overwhelming affection creates a deep emotional bond, making the victim feel special and uniquely valued. However, this idealization is a facade designed to draw the victim in and make them emotionally dependent.

The next phase, devaluation, is marked by a stark shift in the narcissist's behavior. The once adoring partner becomes critical, dismissive, and emotionally abusive. Compliments turn into insults, and supportive gestures become acts of control. The narcissist begins to pick apart the victim's flaws, real or imagined, and uses them as ammunition to undermine their self-esteem. This phase is confusing and painful as the victim struggles to understand why their once-perfect partner has turned against them. The emotional highs of the idealization phase are replaced with crushing lows, leaving the victim desperate to return to the initial stage of the relationship.

Finally, the discard phase occurs when the narcissist decides they no longer need their current source of supply. This phase can be abrupt and brutal, with the narcissist ending the relationship without warning or explanation. They may ghost the victim, cut off all communication, or engage in a dramatic breakup. The victim is left feeling abandoned, worthless, and blindsided. The sudden end to the relationship can be devastating, as the victim grapples with the loss of the idealized love they once had and the harsh reality of the narcissist's true nature.

The psychological impact of these stages is profound. During the idealization phase, the victim experiences emotional highs, feeling loved and cherished. This creates a powerful attachment to the narcissist, making it difficult to see their flaws. In the devaluation phase, the victim's self-esteem is systematically eroded, leading to increased dependency on the narcissist for validation. The alternating periods of affection and abuse create a state of confusion and cognitive dissonance, where the victim struggles to reconcile their partner's loving and cruel behaviors. The discard phase leaves the victim feeling devastated and betrayed, often questioning their worth and reality.

Narcissists repeat this cycle to maintain control and dominance over their partners. The idealization phase ensures the victim becomes emotionally invested, making them easier to manipulate. The devaluation phase keeps the victim off-balance, dependent on the narcissist for any semblance of affection. The discard phase allows the narcissist to move on to new sources of supply, leaving the victim in a state of emotional turmoil. This cycle of abuse serves the narcissist's need for validation and control, perpetuating a continuous loop of idealization, devaluation, and discard.

Consider the case of Lisa, who experienced this cycle multiple times with her narcissistic partner. In the beginning, her partner was charming and attentive, making her feel like the center of his world. As time went on, he began to criticize her appearance, belittle her achievements, and isolate her from friends and family. Despite these red flags, Lisa clung to the memory of their initial love, hoping things would improve. Lisa was left heartbroken and confused when her partner abruptly ended the relationship. Months later, he reappeared, expressing regret and promising to change. The cycle began anew, each iteration leaving Lisa more emotionally battered and dependent.

Long-term relationships with narcissists often follow this pattern. The cycle of abuse keeps the victim in a state of emotional turmoil, making it difficult to break free. The constant shifts between affection and abuse create a powerful bond, where the victim becomes addicted to the highs and lows of the relationship. Recognizing this cycle and understanding its impact is the first step towards breaking free and reclaiming one's life.

The Role of Narcissistic Supply in Relationships

Narcissistic supply is a term used to describe the attention, admiration, and validation that narcissists crave to maintain their inflated self-image. Originating from psychoanalytic theory, the concept of narcissistic supply outlines how individuals with Narcissistic Personality Disorder (NPD) depend on external sources to bolster their self-esteem and sense of worth. This supply is crucial for narcissists, as it temporarily masks their deep-seated insecurities and fragile self-esteem. Without it, they risk confronting the emptiness beneath their grandiose facade.

There are different types of narcissistic supply, each serving a specific purpose. Attention is perhaps the most obvious form. Whether positive or negative, attention feeds the narcissist's ego and keeps them at the center of others' focus. Admiration is another key component. Narcissists thrive on praise and adoration, using it to reinforce their sense of superiority. Validation is equally important, as it confirms their self-perceived exceptionalism and justifies their entitled behavior. These forms of supply are sought after through various manipulative tactics designed to ensure a steady stream of ego-boosting interactions.

Narcissists employ a range of tactics to secure and maintain their supply. Manipulation and charm are their primary tools. They often present themselves as charismatic, engaging, and caring individuals, making drawing others into their orbit easy. This charm can be intoxicating, luring you into a false sense of security and affection. Once you're emotionally invested, the narcissist has a reliable source of supply at their disposal.

Another common strategy is creating dependency. By isolating you from friends and family, the narcissist makes you more reliant on their approval and attention. This isolation can be subtle, starting with minor criticisms of your loved ones and gradually escalating to outright demands for loyalty. Over time, this dependency deepens, ensuring that the narcissist remains the primary source of emotional and social support in your life.

When their supply is threatened or removed, narcissists often react with rage and retaliation. The sudden loss of attention and validation triggers a deep sense of insecurity and vulnerability. In response, the narcissist may lash out, using anger and aggression to reassert control. This rage can be frightening and unpredictable, aimed at punishing you for withdrawing your support.

Attempts to re-establish control are also common. Narcissists may employ hoovering tactics, such as overwhelming you with apologies, promises of change, and declarations of love, to draw you back into the relationship. These tactics are designed to regain your trust and reinstate the flow of supply. However, once you're back in their grasp, the cycle of abuse often resumes.

Consider the example of David, who was married to a narcissistic partner for over a decade. Whenever David tried to assert his independence or spend time with friends, his partner would react with intense anger and manipulation. She would accuse him of neglecting her, creating a scene that left David feeling guilty and isolated. On one occasion, when David decided to attend a family gathering without her, she retaliated by spreading false rumors about him to their mutual friends. This smear campaign was her way of reasserting control and punishing David for seeking validation outside of their relationship.

In another instance, a woman named Carla found herself constantly criticized and belittled by her narcissistic boyfriend. Whenever she received praise at work or compliments from friends, he would downplay her achievements and shift the focus back to himself. If Carla tried to set boundaries or distance herself, he would respond with a mix of rage and desperate attempts to win her back. His need for constant admiration and validation drove him to manipulate Carla's emotions, ensuring that she remained a steady source of narcissistic supply.

Understanding the concept of narcissistic supply is crucial for recognizing the dynamics at play in your relationship. By identifying the tactics used to secure and maintain this supply, you can begin to see through the manipulation and take steps to protect yourself. Acknowledging the impact of losing supply on the narcissist can also prepare you for the potential fallout when you decide to assert your independence. Recognizing these patterns empowers you to break free from the cycle of abuse and reclaim your sense of self-worth.

Chapter Two

Preparing for the Legal Battle

When Lisa decided to divorce her husband, she felt overwhelmed and unsure where to begin. Her husband, a textbook narcissist, had manipulated her for years, leaving her emotionally drained and vulnerable. Lisa knew that divorcing him would be a high-conflict process, fraught with legal battles and emotional turmoil. She needed to prepare herself emotionally and legally to face the challenges ahead. This chapter aims to guide you through the process of gathering evidence, building a strong case, and understanding the legal landscape you'll navigate.

Gathering Evidence of Emotional Abuse

Gathering concrete evidence of emotional abuse is crucial when divorcing a narcissist. Judges and courts rely on tangible proof to make informed decisions, especially in high-conflict cases. Without solid evidence, it becomes challenging to counter the narcissist's manipulative tactics and present a compelling case. Emotional abuse is often subtle and insidious, making it imperative to document every instance meticulously. This documentation will serve as your armor in court, helping you protect your rights and secure a favorable outcome.

Several types of evidence can be used to demonstrate emotional abuse. Text messages and emails are valuable as they provide written records of abusive language, threats, and manipulative behavior. These records can reveal patterns of control and hostility that verbal accounts alone may not capture. Recorded phone conversations can also be powerful, though it's essential to consider the legalities surrounding recording conversations in your jurisdiction. In some states, both parties must consent to being recorded; in others, only one party's consent is necessary. Ensure you understand the laws in your area before proceeding with this method.

Witness testimonies from friends and family who have observed the narcissist's behavior can further corroborate your claims. These testimonies add credibility to your case by providing third-party perspectives on the abuse. Medical and psychological records can also be instrumental. If you have sought therapy or medical treatment due to the stress and trauma caused by the relationship, these records can substantiate your claims of emotional abuse. They provide a professional assessment of the impact the narcissist's behavior has had on your mental and physical health.

Documenting instances of emotional abuse requires diligence and organization. Start by keeping a detailed journal of incidents. Note the date, time, and context of each abusive episode. Describe the narcissist's behavior, your response, and any witnesses present. This journal will serve as a chronological record of the abuse, highlighting patterns and providing context for isolated incidents. Saving and organizing electronic communications is equally important. Create folders for text messages, emails, and other digital interactions. Label these folders by date or topic to make retrieval easier when needed. Keep and document everything!

Legal considerations for evidence collection are paramount. As mentioned earlier, recording conversations must be done within the bounds of the law. Ensure that any evidence you collect is admissible in court. Evidence obtained illegally can be dismissed, weakening your case and potentially leading to legal repercussions. Work closely with your lawyer to understand the legal framework surrounding evidence collection in your jurisdiction. They can guide you on the best practices for gathering and presenting your evidence, ensuring it holds up under scrutiny.

Case Study: Effective Documentation

Consider the case of Emma, who meticulously documented her husband's emotional abuse. She kept a detailed journal, saved every abusive text message, and sought therapy to cope with the trauma. Emma also recorded phone conversations, ensuring she adhered to her state's legal requirements. Her therapist provided a written statement on the psychological impact of the abuse, adding weight to her claims. When Emma presented her evidence in court, the judge had a comprehensive view of the abuse she endured. This thorough documentation helped Emma secure a favorable custody arrangement and financial support, underscoring the importance of diligent evidence collection.

By understanding the significance of evidence and how to gather it effectively, you can build a strong case against your narcissistic partner. This preparation protects your legal interests and empowers you to take control of your situation.

Choosing the Right Lawyer with Experience in NPD Cases

Selecting the right lawyer is a critical step when divorcing a narcissist. This process demands specialized legal representation, as a lawyer familiar with narcissistic behavior can anticipate the manipulative tactics your ex might use in court. A lawyer well-versed in dealing with narcissists understands the intricate dynamics at play, including the psychological manipulation and gaslighting you have endured. This knowledge allows them to build a strong, strategic case that counters the narcissist's attempts to distort reality and undermine your credibility. Choosing a lawyer with this expertise increases your chances of achieving a favorable outcome in custody and divorce proceedings.

When looking for a lawyer, several key qualities and qualifications should be at the top of your list. Experience with high-conflict divorces is paramount, as these cases often involve intense legal battles and emotional strain. A lawyer with a proven track record in similar cases will know how to navigate the complexities and anticipate the narcissist's moves. Strong communication skills are also crucial. Your lawyer should be able to explain legal concepts clearly, keep you informed about your case, and articulate your position effectively in court. Empathy and understanding are equally important. A lawyer who genuinely cares about your well-being and understands the emotional toll of divorcing a narcissist can provide the support and reassurance you need during this challenging time.

During consultations, asking the right questions can help determine if the lawyer is a good fit. Inquire about their experience with cases involving narcissistic personalities and emotional abuse. Ask how they handle high-conflict divorces and what strategies they use against manipulative ex-partners. Questions like "How do you approach custody battles with a manipulative ex?" and "Can you provide references from similar cases?" can give you insight into their expertise and approach. These questions will help you gauge whether the lawyer has the necessary skills and experience to handle your case effectively.

Evaluating potential lawyers requires careful consideration. Start by checking client testimonials and reviews to get a sense of their reputation and client satisfaction. Assess their responsiveness and availability during the consultation. A lawyer who is attentive and readily available to answer your questions will likely be reliable and supportive throughout the legal process. Consider their proposed legal strategy and fees, ensuring they align with your needs and budget. Go through their references to verify their experience and success in similar cases. By thoroughly vetting potential lawyers, you can choose someone who will be a strong advocate for your interests.

The role of your lawyer in a high-conflict divorce extends beyond legal representation. They will act as your advocate in court, presenting your case and countering the narcissist's manipulative tactics. As an advisor, they will guide you through legal strategies, helping you make informed decisions at every stage. Additionally, your lawyer can provide emotional support and guidance, offering reassurance and understanding as you navigate this stressful process. Their multifaceted role is crucial in ensuring you feel supported and empowered throughout the divorce proceedings.

Finding specialized legal support can seem daunting, but several resources can help you locate lawyers experienced in NPD cases. Legal directories and bar associations often have listings of lawyers with specific expertise. Recommendations from support groups and therapists can also be valuable. These professionals often have networks of trusted legal experts who understand the complexities of divorcing a narcissist. By leveraging these resources, you can find a lawyer who is experienced and prepared to handle your case and provide the specialized support you need.

In summary, choosing the right lawyer when divorcing a narcissist is crucial for navigating the legal challenges ahead. Look for someone with experience in high-conflict divorces, strong communication skills, and a deep understanding of narcissistic behavior. Ask pertinent questions during consultations, evaluate potential lawyers carefully, and utilize available resources to find specialized legal support. With the right lawyer, you can build a strong case, protect your interests, and work towards a favorable outcome in your divorce proceedings.

Documenting Interactions and Manipulative Behavior

Thorough documentation is your best ally in legal battles with a narcissist. It serves multiple purposes: building a strong case and protecting yourself from false accusations. Narcissists are adept at twisting the truth, making it crucial for you to have concrete records to counter their manipulative tactics. Judges and courts rely on tangible evidence to make informed decisions. Without proper documentation, your claims may be dismissed as mere allegations, weakening your case and leaving you vulnerable.

Practical methods for documenting interactions and manipulative behaviors include using apps to record conversations, keeping detailed logs and journals, and backing up emails and text messages. Several apps are designed specifically for recording conversations, providing a secure and organized way to capture verbal interactions. However, always check the legalities of recording conversations in your jurisdiction. Keeping a detailed log or journal is another effective method. Write down every instance of abuse, including the date, time, and specific details of what occurred. This log will serve as a chronological record of the narcissist's behavior, making it easier to identify patterns and present them in court. Backing up emails and text messages is equally important. Create folders for these communications, labeling them by date or topic for easy retrieval.

Knowing what to document is as important as knowing how to document. Keep records of threats and abusive language, as these can demonstrate the narcissist's hostile and controlling behavior. Document attempts at manipulation or coercion, such as pressuring you to make decisions against your will or undermining your confidence. Instances of gaslighting or lying should also be meticulously recorded. Note any inconsistencies in their statements or actions, as these can reveal their tendency to distort reality. If the police were involved in any domestic matters, get a copy of the police report(s). This is valuable information for the court to see. Make copies of the police report and give one to your attorney. This comprehensive documentation will provide a robust foundation for your legal case, showcasing the narcissist's true nature.

Organizing and presenting your documentation effectively in court is crucial for its impact. Start by creating a chronological timeline of all documented incidents. This timeline will help the judge see the progression and frequency of the abuse, making it harder for the narcissist to dismiss your claims. Categorize evidence by type, such as verbal abuse, manipulation, and gaslighting. This categorization allows for a clear and structured presentation, making it easier for the court to understand the different facets of the narcissist's behavior. Work closely with your lawyer to compile and present this evidence. They can guide you on how to structure your documentation, ensuring it is compelling and admissible in court.

Imagine you are in court, presenting your case against a narcissistic ex-partner. The judge asks for specific examples of the abuse you endured. With your well-organized documentation, you can confidently provide detailed accounts of each incident, supported by text messages, emails, and recorded conversations. Your chronological timeline offers a clear picture of the ongoing nature of the abuse, countering any attempts by the narcissist to downplay or deny their behavior. Armed with this comprehensive evidence, your lawyer presents a strong and irrefutable case, increasing your chances of a favorable outcome.

In conclusion, thorough documentation is not just a defensive measure; it is an empowering tool. It allows you to take control of your narrative, presenting a clear and compelling case that exposes the narcissist's manipulative tactics. By diligently recording each interaction and organizing your evidence effectively, you build a robust foundation for your legal battle. This preparation will protect you in court and provide a sense of empowerment, knowing you have taken proactive steps to safeguard your future.

Legal Strategies to Counteract Narcissistic Tactics

When divorcing a narcissist, you must prepare for a range of manipulative legal tactics designed to delay proceedings and discredit you. One common strategy is filing frivolous motions to delay the divorce process. These motions are often baseless but serve to complicate and prolong the proceedings, increasing your emotional and financial stress. Recognizing this tactic can help you stay calm and focused. Instead of getting frustrated, understand that this is a ploy to wear you down. Inform your lawyer immediately so they can swiftly counter these motions, ensuring the process stays on track.

False accusations are another weapon in the narcissist's arsenal. They may accuse you of everything from infidelity to being an unfit parent. These claims are intended to discredit you and shift the focus away from their own behavior. To counter these false accusations, gather and present solid evidence that refutes their claims. This could include emails, text messages, and witness testimonies demonstrating your integrity and competence. Solid evidence can dismantle their baseless accusations, revealing them as the manipulative tactics they are.

Narcissists are also skilled at manipulating witnesses and evidence. They may try to coerce mutual friends or family members to testify against you or twist facts to suit their narrative. Preparing your witnesses is crucial. Coach them on what to expect and ensure they understand the importance of sticking to the facts. Your lawyer can also help by conducting mock testimonies so witnesses feel confident and prepared. This preparation can significantly affect how credible and reliable your witnesses appear in court.

Working closely with your legal team is vital. Regular strategy meetings allow you and your lawyer to stay aligned and adapt to new developments. Clear communication ensures that you are both on the same page, reducing the chances of misunderstandings or missed opportunities. Your lawyer can provide updates and adjustments to your strategy based on the narcissist's latest tactics. This collaboration ensures you are always one step ahead, ready to counter manipulative moves.

Maintaining composure in court is another critical aspect of your legal strategy. Narcissists thrive on chaos and emotional reactions. By staying calm and composed, you undermine their attempts to provoke you. Practicing mindfulness and stress-relief techniques can help you manage your emotions. Simple exercises like deep breathing or visualizing a peaceful place can reduce anxiety and keep you focused. Staying centered allows you to present your case clearly and confidently, emphasizing facts and evidence over emotional reactions.

Focusing on facts and evidence is crucial when facing a manipulative ex in court. Narcissists often rely on emotional manipulation and distorted narratives to sway opinions. You build a strong, credible case by consistently presenting clear, factual evidence. Avoid engaging in emotional arguments or getting drawn into their drama. Instead, let the evidence speak for itself. This approach strengthens your case and demonstrates your reliability and integrity to the judge.

Imagine you are in court, and the narcissist has just made a false accusation against you. Instead of reacting emotionally, you calmly present an email thread that disproves their claim. Your lawyer follows up with a well-prepared witness who confirms your version of events. The narcissist's attempt to discredit you falls flat, and their credibility takes a hit. This scenario illustrates the power of preparation, evidence, and composure. By staying focused and working closely with your legal team, you can effectively counter the narcissist's tactics and navigate the legal battle with confidence and resilience.

Navigating Custody Battles with a Narcissist

Custody battles with a narcissist present unique and daunting challenges. One of the most pernicious tactics they employ is parental alienation, where they manipulate your children to turn against you. This can involve badmouthing you, creating false narratives, or even rewarding the children for siding with them. The aim is to undermine your relationship with your kids and paint themselves as the more favorable parent. Additionally, false accusations of unfitness are common. The narcissist might claim you're mentally unstable or unfit to parent, fabricating evidence to support these lies. These accusations are not only distressing but can also jeopardize your custody rights if not effectively countered.

Manipulating children to gain leverage is another tactic. Narcissists often use their children as pawns, manipulating their emotions to control the narrative. They might tell the children lies about you, making them believe that you are the cause of the family's problems. This emotional manipulation can be deeply damaging to the children, creating confusion and conflict in their minds. Protecting your parental rights in such a scenario requires a proactive and strategic approach. Seeking custody evaluations and psychological assessments can provide an objective view of the family dynamics. These evaluations are conducted by professionals who can identify signs of manipulation and provide an unbiased assessment to the court.

Documenting all interactions with your children is equally crucial. Keep a detailed record of your time together, noting dates, activities, and any notable conversations. This documentation can demonstrate your involvement and commitment as a parent, countering any claims of neglect or disinterest. Building a strong case for custody involves gathering evidence of your parental involvement and care. Collect school reports, medical records, and other documents that show your active participation in your children's lives. Demonstrating the narcissist's manipulative and abusive behavior is also vital. This can include witness testimonies, recorded conversations (if legally permissible), and any other evidence that exposes their true nature.

Involving child therapists and counselors can provide additional support. These professionals can offer insights into the emotional well-being of your children and the impact of the narcissist's behavior. Their assessments and testimonies can be powerful tools in court, highlighting the need for a stable and nurturing environment. Preparing for court appearances requires meticulous planning. Work closely with your lawyer to anticipate the narcissist's tactics. Practice your testimony and responses, focusing on clear, concise, factual statements. Rehearsing with your lawyer can help you stay calm and composed under pressure, ensuring you present your case effectively.

Ensuring all documentation and evidence are organized and ready is paramount. Create a comprehensive file with all relevant documents categorized and labeled for easy access. This organization helps you stay prepared and demonstrates your thoroughness and credibility to the court. As you navigate this challenging process, remember that your primary goal is to protect your children's well-being. Your efforts to gather evidence, seek professional assessments, and build a strong case are all steps toward ensuring a safe and supportive environment for them.

By understanding the unique challenges of custody battles with a narcissist and employing strategic measures to counteract their tactics, you can protect your parental rights and safeguard your children's future. Your diligence and determination will be instrumental in navigating this complex legal landscape and securing a favorable outcome for your family.

Guardian ad Litem (GAL)

A GAL is a court-appointed individual, often an attorney or trained professional, whose primary role is to represent the best interests of a child(ren) in legal matters, particularly custody disputes. When dealing with a narcissistic co-parent in a custody case, having a GAL can be incredibly beneficial. Narcissists are often skilled at manipulation, creating an environment where facts are distorted and emotional abuse is subtle yet damaging. A GAL serves as an impartial party, investigating the situation by speaking with both parents, the child(ren), and sometimes other involved parties like teachers or counselors. Their goal is to present an unbiased report to the court, ensuring that the child's needs, rather than the narcissistic parent's agenda, are the central focus.

You can **request a Guardian ad Litem** if you believe that your custody case is particularly complex or involves concerns about the child's well-being. In some cases, the court may also appoint a GAL on its own, particularly if there are accusations of abuse, neglect, or high-conflict situations where it's difficult to discern the child's best interests. The GAL provides the court with valuable insight, especially in cases where a narcissistic parent may attempt to discredit the other parent or control the narrative. The presence of a GAL helps mitigate these tactics by offering an independent, fact-based evaluation that supports a fair outcome for the child.

In some situations, it is possible to **request that the other party be responsible for covering the costs** of the GAL. This can be particularly relevant when dealing with a narcissistic parent, as they may use financial pressure as a tactic to manipulate or prolong the legal process. Asking the court to have the narcissist bear the financial responsibility for the GAL can help level the playing field, ensuring that the process remains focused on the child's best interests without undue financial stress on the other party. Ultimately, a GAL can be a powerful ally in navigating the complexities of custody disputes involving a narcissist, offering both protection and advocacy for the child.

A final word on all of this: document, document, and document. It matters. Use a reliable app that timestamps. Time-stamping entries is crucial when dealing with the court system because they provide a clear and verifiable record of when specific events or actions took place. It also establishes a history of abuse and manipulation that will be powerful for the Court to see. Some popular apps for widely used time-stamping are DocuSign, Evernote, Day One, Diarium, Penzu, and Notarize. Also, you should document your stability and involvement in your children's lives. Document when and how frequently you volunteer at your children's schools. Document if you coach any sports activities or host any clubs. Are you on any committees at your children's school? If so, document it. Showing a pattern of being an involved and caring parent over the years can go a long way in a courtroom to show your dedication to your children and your stabilizing influence.

The next chapter will explore the critical aspects of creating a safety plan to protect yourself and your children during this tumultuous time.

Chapter Three

Creating a Safety Plan

When Jane finally decided to leave her narcissistic husband, she knew it wouldn't be easy. For years, she had endured his manipulation, his constant belittling, and his gaslighting. She was not as confident as she used to be and was very scared of her husband. She was not feeling strong; she often felt weak and hopeless. She feared the mental warfare he would unleash upon her when she tried to leave. To say she felt intimidated, frightened, and overwhelmed would be the understatement of the year. But the moment she found herself fearing for her mental and physical safety, she realized it was time to plan her exit. She could not live her life this way. Jane's story is not unique; many who find themselves in relationships with narcissists face the same challenges. Understanding the importance of a meticulously crafted safety plan can be the difference between a smooth transition to a new life and a dangerous escalation of abuse.

Planning Your Safe Exit

The importance of a detailed exit plan cannot be overstated when you're in a relationship with a narcissist. Narcissists thrive on control; the moment they sense they are losing their grip, they can become unpredictable and even dangerous. Having a safe exit plan reduces the risk of immediate retaliation. The narcissist will likely react strongly to the loss of their primary source of narcissistic supply, and this reaction can range from emotional manipulation to physical aggression. Planning your exit carefully can mitigate these risks and ensure a smoother transition to a new living situation.

Creating a safe exit plan involves several crucial steps. First, you need to identify the best time and method for leaving. Timing is critical; choosing a moment when the narcissist is least likely to suspect or resist your departure can significantly reduce the risk of confrontation. This might be when they are at work, out of town, or otherwise preoccupied. The method of leaving should be discreet and well-organized. I strongly recommend enlisting the help of trusted friends or family members to assist with the move and provide emotional support. Another consideration, if you have children, is whether or not to tell the children's school(s) about the situation. This is a personal choice dependent upon your specific circumstances. Notifying the school(s) is good in that it will have teachers and support staff prepared for any outbursts from your narcissist, and you can also ask them to keep an extra eye on your children to see if they are showing signs of distress.

Preparing an emergency bag with essentials is another vital step. This bag should include important documents, such as identification, financial records, legal paperwork, and personal items like clothing, medications, and any necessities for children or pets. Having this bag ready in advance ensures you can leave quickly if the situation suddenly becomes unsafe. Consider keeping this bag at a trusted friend's house. That way, if you absolutely have to go in a rush you can leave, get to a safe place, and then collect your emergency bag from your friend. Additionally, inform trusted friends or family members about your plan. They can offer support, provide a temporary place to stay, and help you coordinate your move. Ensure they understand the situation's seriousness and the need for discretion. Only confide your plans with people you absolutely trust with your life. It would be terrible to share your plan with someone who then betrayed you and told your narcissist of your plans.

Emergency preparation is critical for handling unexpected situations. Having a list of emergency contacts and hotlines can provide quick access to help if needed. Include contacts for local law enforcement, domestic violence hotlines, and nearby emergency shelters. Knowing where to go if immediate danger arises is also essential. Identify safe locations, such as the homes of trusted friends or family members, where you can seek refuge. Domestic violence shelters can offer temporary housing and additional resources to support you during this transition.

Coordination with authorities can provide an additional layer of safety. Notify local police about your situation and your plans to leave. This can ensure a faster response time if you need assistance. Obtaining a restraining order or protective order can legally prevent the narcissist from approaching you, providing a measure of security and peace of mind. These legal protections can be crucial in cases where the narcissist has a history of physical violence or threats.

If children are involved, you must first consult with a lawyer. Taking the children and removing them from the family home is going to enrage your narcissist and will most likely result in your narcissist lashing out. Your narcissist will know your most vulnerable area is your children, and that is where they will look to manipulate you. I am sure they have already played that card with you many times to keep you and manipulate you. Now, they will ramp that up tenfold and may try to involve the police. It is imperative you consult with a lawyer who has experience in high-conflict divorce and narcissism and find out the laws in your state regarding removing the children from the family home. If you are working with a therapist, involve the therapist in these plans. You want to make sure you have solid legal grounds, therapist involvement, and that the interests and safety of the kids are prioritized.

Checklist for Your Safe Exit Plan

- Identify a Safe Time and Method for Leaving:
    - Choose a time when the narcissist is least likely to notice.
    - Plan your exit strategy and rehearse if necessary.
- Prepare an Emergency Bag:
    - Include important documents (ID, financial records, legal paperwork).
    - Pack clothing, medications, and personal items.
    - Items for children or pets are.
- Inform Trusted Friends or Family Members:
    - Share your plan with a few trusted individuals.
    - Arrange for temporary housing if needed.
    - Request their assistance during the move.

- Emergency Preparation:

    ◦ List emergency contacts and hotlines.

    ◦ Identify safe locations (friends' homes, shelters).

- Coordinate with Authorities:

    ◦ Notify local police about your situation.

    ◦ Obtain a restraining order or protective order if necessary.

***Inform children's school(s).

You take control of your safety and well-being by meticulously planning your exit. Each step you take towards this plan is a step towards freedom and a new beginning. Remember, you are not alone; support is available to help you navigate this challenging time.

Securing Important Documents and Assets

When preparing to leave a narcissist, securing important documents is vital. These documents are not only crucial for your identity but also for legal and financial proceedings. Start by identifying essential documents that you need to gather and secure. Birth certificates and social security cards for you and your children are fundamental. These documents are required for various legal and administrative purposes, such as enrolling your children in a new school or applying for government assistance. Financial records and bank statements are also critical. These documents provide a comprehensive view of your financial situation, which is essential for divorce proceedings and financial planning.

Additionally, gather legal documents such as marriage certificates, custody papers, court orders, or legal agreements. Be sure to include any documents, records, and reports you have gathered for an attorney in preparation for your divorce. Also, be sure to have all the usernames and passwords for your various accounts (bank, mortgage, investment, email, social media, etc.). These documents will be vital in your legal battle and in securing your rights.

Securing these documents requires careful planning and execution. Start by making copies of all essential documents. This ensures you have a backup in case the originals are lost or destroyed. Store these copies with a trusted person, such as a close friend or family member, who understands the gravity of your situation. Alternatively, you can use a safe deposit box that only you can access at a bank to store these documents securely. Another option is to use secure online storage. Scanning and storing your documents in a secure cloud service provides easy access while safeguarding them against physical loss or tampering. Just make sure you are the only person who can access them.

Protecting your financial assets from being accessed or manipulated by the narcissist is another crucial step. Narcissists often use financial control as a means of maintaining power and dominance. To counter this, open separate bank accounts in your name only. This ensures that your financial resources are under your control and cannot be accessed by the narcissist. Monitoring your credit reports for suspicious activity is also essential. Narcissists may attempt to open credit accounts or make large purchases in your name, damaging your financial standing. Regularly check your credit reports for any unauthorized activity and take immediate action if you notice anything suspicious.

Freezing joint accounts and credit cards is another effective measure to protect your financial assets. Contact your bank and credit card companies to inform them of your situation and request that joint accounts be frozen. This prevents the narcissist from making withdrawals or charges without your consent. Additionally, consider setting up alerts on your accounts to notify you of any transactions. This provides an extra layer of security and allows you to act quickly if any unauthorized activity occurs.

Legal protections for assets are also available and can provide additional security during the separation process. Filing for temporary financial orders can legally restrict the narcissist from accessing joint accounts or selling shared assets. These orders can also mandate spousal and child support payments, ensuring you have the financial resources needed during the divorce process. Consulting with a financial advisor or attorney is highly recommended. These professionals can provide expert advice on protecting your assets and navigating the complex financial landscape of divorce. They can help you understand your rights, develop a financial plan, and take legal steps to secure your financial future.

Consider the example of Maria, who was in the process of divorcing her narcissistic husband. She made copies of all her important documents and stored them with her sister. She also scanned these documents and saved them in a secure online folder. Maria opened a separate bank account and redirected her paycheck to this new account, ensuring her financial resources were protected. She monitored her credit reports and froze joint accounts, preventing her husband from making unauthorized transactions. Additionally, Maria worked with a lawyer and the bank to file for temporary financial orders, securing spousal support and protecting her assets during the divorce proceedings.

By taking these steps, you can safeguard your important documents and financial assets, ensuring you have the resources and legal protection needed during this challenging time. This preparation protects your legal and financial interests and provides peace of mind, knowing that you have taken proactive steps to secure your future.

Finding Safe Housing and Emergency Contacts

When you're preparing to leave a narcissist, identifying safe housing options is a critical step. Domestic violence shelters offer immediate refuge and are designed to provide both safety and support. These shelters often have security measures in place to protect you from being found by your abuser. They also offer resources such as counseling, legal aid, and support groups, which can be invaluable during this transitional period. Another option is staying with trusted family or friends. This can provide a safe place to stay and emotional support from people who care about you. Make sure that the people you choose to stay with understand the seriousness of the situation and are prepared to offer the necessary support and discretion. Temporary housing programs are another viable option. These programs can provide short-term housing solutions while you work on finding a more permanent solution. Non-profit organizations and community services often run these programs, providing additional support and resources to help you get back on your feet.

Preparing for the move to safe housing requires careful planning and discretion. Start by discreetly packing your belongings. Choose times when the narcissist is not around to avoid raising suspicion. Pack essential items first, such as clothing, toiletries, and any personal items you can't live without. Use unmarked boxes or bags to avoid drawing attention. Arrange transportation in advance. Whether you're using your own vehicle or relying on a friend or family member, make sure the transportation is readily available when you're ready to leave. This minimizes the time spent in a vulnerable position and ensures a swift, efficient move.

Creating an emergency contact list is another crucial step in your safety plan. This list should include local law enforcement and domestic violence hotlines. Having these numbers readily available ensures you can quickly access help if needed. Trusted friends and family members should also be on this list. These are the people you can call in an emergency or for immediate support. Legal and medical professionals should also be included. Your lawyer's contact information is essential for any legal emergencies, while medical professionals can provide assistance if you or your children need medical care. Keep this list in an easily accessible place, such as your phone or a small notebook that you carry with you.

Establishing a support network is vital for ongoing safety and emotional support. Joining support groups and online communities can provide a sense of belonging and understanding. These groups are often filled with people who have gone through similar experiences and can offer advice, support, and a listening ear. Connecting with advocacy organizations can also be beneficial. These organizations often provide resources, legal aid, and emotional support to help you navigate the challenges of leaving a narcissist. They can also connect you with other survivors, providing a sense of community and shared experience.

Here are suggestions for your emergency contacts. Please ensure you have all of these names, numbers, and contacts and that they are easily and readily available.

- Local Law Enforcement:

    - Police Department
    - Domestic Violence Unit
- Domestic Violence Hotlines:
    - National Domestic Violence Hotline
    - Local Shelter Hotline:
- Trusted Friends and Family Members:
- Legal and Medical Professionals:
    - Lawyer
    - Therapist
    - Primary Care Doctor

By taking these steps, you're preparing for your immediate safety and laying the groundwork for long-term stability and support. Each element of your plan is a building block toward a safer, more secure future. Remember, you don't have to do this alone. There are resources and people ready to support you every step of the way.

Protecting Yourself from Physical and Emotional Retaliation

Understanding the risks associated with leaving a narcissist is crucial. Narcissists often escalate their abusive behavior when they feel their control slipping away. This can manifest as physical aggression or heightened emotional manipulation. They might attempt to coerce you into staying by making threats or promising to change. These tactics are designed to instill fear and uncertainty, making you question your decision to leave. Recognizing these risks allows you to take proactive steps to protect yourself from immediate and future harm.

Enhancing your physical safety starts with securing your new home. Installing security systems, such as alarms and surveillance cameras, can provide an additional layer of protection. These systems act as a deterrent and offer peace of mind, knowing that any unauthorized attempts to enter your home will trigger an alert. Upgrading the locks and securing all of the windows are simple yet effective measures. Ensure all entry points are fortified with solid locks and that windows have safety latches. This prevents the narcissist from gaining easy access to your new living space.

Carrying personal safety devices, like pepper spray or a personal alarm, can also enhance your security. These devices are easy to use and can provide a quick defense if you find yourself in a threatening situation. Always keep them within reach, whether at home or in public. Familiarize yourself with how they work so you can use them effectively if needed. Remember, these devices are tools to buy you time to escape or call for help, not to engage in a physical confrontation.

Emotional safety is just as important as physical safety. Regular therapy or counseling sessions can provide a safe space to process your emotions and develop coping strategies. A therapist can help you navigate the complex feelings of guilt, fear, and confusion that often accompany leaving a narcissist. They can also offer techniques to manage stress and build resilience. Practicing mindfulness and relaxation techniques, such as deep breathing exercises or meditation, can help you stay grounded and calm. These practices reduce anxiety and improve your overall emotional well-being.

Setting firm boundaries is crucial for maintaining your emotional safety. Clearly communicate what behaviors are unacceptable and stick to these boundaries. Practicing "no contact" is often the most effective way to enforce these boundaries. This means cutting off all forms of communication with the narcissist, including phone calls, texts, and social media interactions. If complete no contact is not possible due to shared responsibilities, such as co-parenting, limit interactions to necessary communications and keep them strictly business-like.

Legal protections against retaliation are available and can offer significant peace of mind. Filing for restraining orders or protective orders can legally prevent the narcissist from coming near you or contacting you. These orders are enforceable by law, and violating them can result in legal consequences for the narcissist. Documenting any threats or incidents is crucial for obtaining these legal protections. Keep a detailed record of any threatening messages, emails, or encounters. This documentation serves as evidence to support your request for a restraining order and can also be used in future legal proceedings if necessary.

Understanding the potential for escalation and taking proactive steps to enhance both your physical and emotional safety is essential when leaving a narcissist. By securing your new home, carrying personal safety devices, and seeking regular therapy, you create a protective environment for yourself. Setting firm boundaries and practicing no contact help maintain your emotional well-being, while legal protections provide additional security. Documenting threats and incidents ensures you have the necessary evidence to support your legal actions. Each of these steps is a crucial component of your safety plan, helping you transition to a safer, more stable life free from the narcissist's control.

Chapter Four

Financial Independence and Recovery

When Melissa finally decided to leave her narcissistic husband, she was overwhelmed by the financial complexities ahead. For years, her husband had controlled their finances, leaving her in the dark about their financial situation. She had no idea where to start or how to secure her financial independence. Melissa's story is a common one. Many people in relationships with narcissists find themselves financially entangled and unprepared for the challenges that come with divorce. This chapter aims to guide you through the process of regaining control of your finances, ensuring you have the knowledge and tools to rebuild your financial stability.

Regaining Control of Your Finances

Assessing your financial situation is the first and most crucial step in regaining control. Understanding where you stand financially allows you to make informed decisions and create a plan that addresses your immediate needs and long-term goals. Start by creating an inventory of assets and liabilities. List all your assets, including bank accounts, real estate, investments, and personal property. Then, identify your liabilities, such as mortgages, loans, credit card debt, and any other financial obligations. This inventory provides a clear picture of your net worth and helps you understand what resources you have at your disposal.

Next, review your bank statements and credit reports. Bank statements offer insights into your spending habits, income sources, and any recurring expenses. Analyzing these statements helps you identify areas where you can cut costs and allocate funds more effectively. Credit reports, on the other hand, provide a comprehensive view of your credit history. They detail your credit accounts, outstanding debts, and credit score. Regularly reviewing your credit reports allows you to spot any inaccuracies or fraudulent activities that need to be addressed. Identifying your sources of income and expenses is also essential. List all your income sources, such as salary, alimony, child support, and any side income. Then, categorize your expenses into fixed (e.g., rent, utilities) and variable (e.g., groceries, entertainment). This breakdown helps you understand your cash flow and identify areas where you can make adjustments to improve your financial health.

Separating joint finances is a critical step in disentangling yourself from your narcissistic ex. It is crucial to speak with a divorce attorney before doing anything. Laws vary from state to state, so you must consult a divorce attorney to see what you can do to separate your joint assets legally. Joint accounts are usually most vulnerable before official divorce proceedings are filed with the court. Once divorce papers have been filed with the courts, injunctions usually prevent both parties from withdrawing and transferring funds from joint accounts. Again, you must consult with a divorce attorney in your state and learn what is allowed there.

You will want to open an individual account. Redirecting direct deposits and automatic payments to your individual account is another crucial step. Ensure that your salary and any other income are deposited into your individual account. Update any automatic payments, such as utilities and subscriptions, to be debited from your new account. This step prevents your ex from accessing your funds and ensures you have control over your expenses.

Refinancing joint loans and mortgages is also important. Joint loans and mortgages can be a source of financial entanglement and conflict. Contact your lender to discuss refinancing options that allow you to remove your ex's name from the loan or mortgage. This step ensures that you are solely responsible for the debt and prevents your ex from using it as leverage. If refinancing is not an option, consider selling the property and dividing the proceeds to eliminate the shared financial burden.

Creating a financial action plan is essential for addressing your immediate financial needs and setting long-term goals. Start by setting short-term and long-term financial goals. Short-term goals might include paying off credit card debt, building an emergency fund, or saving for a specific expense. Long-term goals could involve saving for retirement, buying a home, or funding your children's education. Prioritizing debt repayment and savings is crucial. Focus on paying off high-interest debts first, as they can quickly accumulate and become unmanageable. Simultaneously, work on building an emergency fund that can cover at least three to six months of living expenses. This fund provides a financial safety net in case of unexpected expenses or emergencies.

Protecting your credit score is vital during and after a divorce. A good credit score is essential for securing loans, renting apartments, and getting certain jobs. Monitoring your credit reports regularly allows you to spot any inaccuracies or fraudulent activities. Dispute any inaccuracies with the credit bureaus to ensure your credit report accurately reflects your financial history. Avoiding unnecessary debt is also crucial. While relying on credit cards to cover expenses may be tempting, accumulating more debt can damage your credit score and create financial stress. Focus on living within your means and using credit responsibly.

Action Step: Creating Your Financial Inventory

- List Your Assets:
  - Bank accounts
  - Real estate
  - Investments
  - Personal property
- Identify Your Liabilities:
  - Mortgages
  - Loans
  - Credit card debt

- Other financial obligations
- Review Bank Statements and Credit Reports:
    - Analyze spending habits and income sources
    - Spot inaccuracies or fraudulent activities
- Identify Income and Expenses:
    - List all income sources
    - Categorize expenses into fixed and variable

By taking these steps, you can regain control of your finances and build a solid foundation for your financial future. Understanding your financial situation, separating joint finances, creating a financial action plan, and protecting your credit score are all essential to achieving financial independence and stability.

Budgeting Tips for Post-Divorce Life

Creating a realistic budget is a fundamental step to regaining financial stability post-divorce. Start by listing all sources of income. This includes your salary, alimony, child support, and any side income you might have. Having a clear picture of your income helps you understand what you have to work with each month. Next, categorize and prioritize your expenses. Divide them into essential and non-essential categories. Essential expenses include housing, utilities, groceries, insurance, and transportation. Non-essential expenses might include dining out, entertainment, and subscription services. Prioritizing these expenses ensures that your basic needs are met first. Setting aside funds for emergency savings is also crucial. Aim to save a small portion of your income each month, even if it's just a little. This emergency fund will provide a financial cushion in case of unexpected expenses, such as car repairs or medical bills.

Cutting unnecessary expenses can free up funds for more important needs and savings. Start by reviewing your subscription services and memberships. Many people pay for multiple streaming services, gym memberships, or other subscriptions they rarely use. Canceling or downgrading these services can save you a significant amount each month. Comparing prices for utilities and insurance is another effective strategy. Shop around for the best electricity, water, and gas rates. The same goes for insurance policies. Contact different providers to get quotes and see if you can find a better deal. Cooking at home instead of dining out is another simple way to save money. Preparing meals at home is often much cheaper than eating at restaurants or ordering takeout. It also allows you to make healthier food choices, which can benefit your overall well-being.

Using budgeting tools and apps can help you manage and track your expenses more effectively. There are several popular budgeting apps available that offer various features to suit your needs. Apps like Mint, YNAB (You Need a Budget), and PocketGuard can help you create a budget, track your spending, and set financial goals. Setting up these tools is usually straightforward. You'll need to link your bank accounts and credit cards to the app, allowing it to automatically track your transactions. You can then categorize your expenses and set spending limits for each category. There are numerous benefits to digital budgeting over traditional methods. These apps provide real-time updates, send alerts when you're nearing your spending limits, and offer insights into your spending habits. They can help you stay on track and make informed financial decisions.

Adjusting to a single income requires practical steps and a mindset shift. Downsizing living arrangements, if necessary, can significantly reduce your expenses. Consider moving to a smaller home or apartment that better fits your budget. This can lower your rent or mortgage payments and reduce utility costs. Finding additional income streams can also help ease the financial burden. Look for part-time jobs, freelance work, or side gigs that align with your skills and interests. Even a small increase in income can make a big difference. Seeking financial assistance programs is another option. Many communities offer support services for single parents, low-income families, and individuals going through a divorce. These programs can provide financial aid, food assistance, and other resources to help you manage your expenses.

Budgeting Exercise: Create Your Monthly Budget

- List Your Income Sources:
    - Salary
    - Alimony
    - Child Support
    - Side Income
- Categorize and Prioritize Expenses:
    - Essential Expenses (housing, utilities, groceries, insurance, transportation)
    - Non-Essential Expenses (dining out, entertainment, subscriptions)

- Set Aside Emergency Savings:
    - Aim to save a small portion of your income each month
- Cut Unnecessary Expenses:
    - Review and cancel unused subscriptions
    - Compare prices for utilities and insurance
    - Cook at home instead of dining out
- Use Budgeting Tools and Apps:
    - Set up a budgeting app (Mint, YNAB, PocketGuard)
    - Link your accounts and categorize expenses
    - Set spending limits and track progress
- Adjust to a Single Income:
    - Downsize living arrangements if necessary
    - Find additional income streams (part-time jobs, freelance work)
    - Seek financial assistance programs

By taking these steps, you can create a realistic budget that reflects your new financial reality post-divorce. Understanding your income and expenses, cutting unnecessary costs, and using modern budgeting tools will help you manage your finances more effectively. Adjusting to a single income may take time and effort, but you can achieve financial stability and independence with careful planning and proactive measures.

Financial Planning for a Secure Future

Setting long-term financial goals is crucial for building a stable future. These goals give you direction and a sense of purpose, helping you stay focused on what matters most. Think about what you want to achieve in the next five, ten, or even twenty years. Common goals include saving for retirement, buying a home, or funding your children's education. Start by creating a timeline for each goal. For example, if you want to buy a home in five years, outline the steps you need to take to reach that goal. This might include saving for a down payment, improving your credit score, and researching mortgage options. Setting clear, achievable milestones makes your long-term goals feel more attainable.

An emergency fund is another critical aspect of financial planning. Life is unpredictable, and having a financial safety net can provide peace of mind and security. Aim to save enough to cover three to six months of living expenses. This fund will help you manage unexpected costs, such as medical bills or car repairs, without derailing your financial plans. Start by determining the ideal amount for your emergency fund. Calculate your monthly expenses, including rent, utilities, groceries, and insurance, and multiply by the number of months you want to cover. Building this fund takes time, so set a consistent contribution goal. Even small, regular deposits can add up over time. Consider automating your savings to ensure you consistently contribute to your emergency fund.

Investing for the future is another key component of financial security. There are various investment options to consider, each with its benefits. Stocks are shares in a company; owning them means you have a stake in that company's success. Stocks can offer high returns, but they also come with higher risks. Bonds are loans you give to companies or governments, which pay you interest over time. They are generally safer than stocks but offer lower returns. Mutual funds pool money from many investors to buy a diversified portfolio of stocks, bonds, or other assets. This diversification can reduce risk. Real estate investments are another option. Owning property can provide rental income and potential appreciation in value. Retirement accounts like 401(k)s and IRAs are designed to help you save for retirement. These accounts offer tax advantages and can be invested in stocks, bonds, and mutual funds. Diversifying your investments can help balance risk and reward, ensuring you have a secure financial future.

Insurance and protection are vital for maintaining financial stability. Life insurance policies provide financial support to your beneficiaries in the event of your death. There are different types of life insurance, including term life and whole life. Term life insurance covers you for a specific period, while whole life insurance provides lifelong coverage and often includes a savings component. Health insurance is essential for covering medical expenses, from routine check-ups to major surgeries. Without health insurance, medical bills can quickly become overwhelming. Disability insurance replaces a portion of your income if you become unable to work due to illness or injury. This coverage can help you maintain your financial stability during challenging times. Property and casualty insurance protect your assets, such as your home and car, from damage or loss. Homeowners or renters insurance covers your home and belongings, while auto insurance covers your vehicle. These policies can help you recover financially from accidents, natural disasters, or theft.

By focusing on setting long-term financial goals, building an emergency fund, investing wisely, and securing appropriate insurance, you can create a solid foundation for a secure financial future. This comprehensive approach ensures that you are prepared for both expected and unexpected events, giving you peace of mind and financial stability as you move forward.

Finding Financial Advisors and Support Groups

The role of a financial advisor can be instrumental in creating and maintaining a financial plan tailored to your unique situation. Financial advisors offer a range of services designed to help you manage your finances effectively. They can assist in budgeting, investment planning, retirement savings, and debt management. By providing professional guidance, they can help you navigate complex financial landscapes, ensuring that you make informed decisions that align with your long-term goals. Financial advisors can also offer personalized advice based on your specific needs and circumstances, helping you build a financial strategy that works for you. The benefits of professional financial guidance are numerous. With an advisor by your side, you gain access to expert knowledge and insights that can help you optimize your financial resources and achieve greater stability.

Choosing the right financial advisor is crucial, especially when recovering from a high-conflict divorce. Look for an advisor with credentials such as Certified Financial Planner (CFP) or Chartered Financial Analyst (CFA). These certifications indicate a high level of expertise and adherence to ethical standards. Experience in handling cases similar to yours is also essential. Ask potential advisors about their experience with clients who have gone through high-conflict divorces and how they have helped them achieve financial stability.

During consultations, ask questions to assess whether the advisor is a good fit for your needs. Inquire about their approach to financial planning, their fee structure, and how they will tailor their services to your situation. Understanding their process and ensuring they are empathetic and supportive can significantly impact your financial recovery.

Joining financial support groups can provide additional benefits as you work towards financial recovery. These groups offer a sense of community and shared experience, which can be incredibly valuable during challenging times. There are various types of financial support groups available, including those specifically focused on individuals recovering from divorce or financial abuse. Some groups meet in person, while others are available online, offering flexibility and convenience. Finding local and online groups is relatively straightforward. Start by searching online for support groups in your area or join forums and social media groups dedicated to financial recovery. Many organizations and non-profits also offer support groups and resources for individuals facing financial challenges.

The benefits of peer support and shared experiences in these groups cannot be overstated. Being part of a community that understands your struggles and can offer practical advice and emotional support can be incredibly empowering. Members of these groups often share tips, resources, and strategies that have worked for them, providing you with a wealth of information and support. Additionally, hearing about others' successes and challenges can offer inspiration and motivation, helping you stay focused on your financial goals. The sense of camaraderie and mutual support in these groups can make a significant difference in your financial recovery journey.

Resources for financial education are abundant and can help you improve your financial literacy and confidence. Books, online courses, and workshops are excellent starting points. Many books cover various aspects of personal finance, from budgeting and saving to investing and retirement planning. Some highly regarded titles include "The Total Money Makeover" by Dave Ramsey and "Your Money or Your Life" by Vicki Robin. Online courses and workshops offer interactive and structured learning experiences. Websites like Coursera, Udemy, and Khan Academy provide courses on personal finance, investment strategies, and financial planning.

Websites and forums dedicated to financial education can also be valuable resources. Websites like Investopedia and NerdWallet offer articles, tutorials, and tools to help you understand financial concepts and make informed decisions. Forums such as Reddit's r/personalfinance and Bogleheads provide platforms for discussion and advice from a community of financially savvy individuals. These resources allow you to learn at your own pace and seek guidance on specific topics as needed. By taking advantage of these educational resources, you can build your financial knowledge and confidence, empowering you to take control of your financial future.

As you continue to rebuild your life after divorcing a narcissist, finding the right financial advisor and support groups can provide invaluable guidance and community. Utilizing resources for financial education further enhances your ability to manage your finances effectively. With the right support and knowledge, you can achieve financial independence and stability, setting the stage for a secure and fulfilling future.

Next, we will focus on the emotional healing and self-care strategies that are just as critical in your journey to recovery and independence.

Chapter Five

Emotional Healing and Self-Care

When Laura finally left her narcissistic husband, she felt a mix of relief and overwhelming anxiety. She had spent years second-guessing her reality, enduring constant emotional turmoil, and feeling trapped in a cycle of manipulation. Now, free from his grasp, she faced the daunting task of rebuilding her sense of self and healing from the trauma. This chapter focuses on individuals like Laura, who are seeking to reclaim their lives and find peace after a tumultuous relationship with a narcissist.

Therapeutic Exercises for Trauma Recovery

Addressing trauma after leaving a narcissistic relationship is crucial for your mental health and overall well-being. Emotional trauma can profoundly affect your mental health, leading to symptoms such as anxiety, depression, and post-traumatic stress disorder (PTSD). The constant manipulation, gaslighting, and emotional abuse can leave you feeling isolated, worthless, and confused. These effects do not disappear overnight; they require deliberate and compassionate effort to heal. Seeking professional help is a vital first step. Therapists experienced in trauma and narcissistic abuse can provide tailored strategies to help you navigate this complex emotional landscape.

Cognitive Behavioral Therapy (CBT) is one of the most effective therapeutic approaches for managing trauma symptoms. CBT focuses on identifying and challenging negative thought patterns that contribute to emotional distress. One useful CBT exercise is keeping thought records. In a thought record, you document negative thoughts as they arise, examine the evidence for and against these thoughts, and then reframe them into more balanced, realistic perspectives. This exercise helps you break the cycle of negative thinking and fosters a healthier mindset. Behavioral activation is another CBT technique that encourages you to engage in positive activities that bring joy and fulfillment. By scheduling and participating in these activities, you can counteract the inertia and withdrawal often associated with depression and trauma.

Somatic experiencing is another powerful method for trauma recovery that focuses on releasing stored trauma from the body. Trauma can manifest physically, creating tension, pain, or a sense of disconnect from your body. Grounding exercises are an effective way to connect with the present moment and your physical sensations. These exercises might include feeling the texture of an object, listening to the sounds around you, or focusing on your breath. Grounding can help you feel more anchored and less overwhelmed by traumatic memories. Body scan meditation is another somatic experiencing technique. In this practice, you slowly scan your body from head to toe, noticing areas of tension or discomfort. By bringing awareness to these areas and practicing relaxation, you can release stored trauma and foster a sense of physical and emotional well-being.

Creative therapies such as art and music therapy offer additional avenues for expressing and processing trauma. These therapies can be particularly beneficial if you struggle to verbalize your experiences. Drawing or painting your emotions allows you to externalize and explore your feelings nonverbally. This creative expression can provide insights into your emotional state and offer a sense of release. Creating a trauma timeline through art is another effective technique. By visually chronicling significant events and their emotional impact, you can gain a clearer understanding of your trauma and its progression. This process can help you identify patterns and triggers, empowering you to address them more effectively. Music therapy uses music to facilitate healing. Listening to or creating music can evoke emotions, memories, and sensations that are often difficult to access through words alone. Music can be a powerful emotional expression and processing tool, providing comfort and connection.

Engaging in these therapeutic exercises can help you manage and reduce the symptoms of trauma. By addressing both the cognitive and somatic aspects of trauma, you can foster a more holistic and integrated healing process. Creative therapies provide additional tools for expression and exploration, offering new pathways to understanding and recovery. Through these practices, you can begin to reclaim your sense of self, rebuild your emotional resilience, and move forward with a renewed sense of hope and empowerment.

Mindfulness Practices for Emotional Stability

Mindfulness is the practice of paying attention to the present moment without judgment. It helps you achieve emotional stability by grounding you in the here and now, reducing anxiety about the future and regrets about the past. Practicing mindfulness regularly can lower stress levels, improve focus, and enhance emotional regulation. When you're mindful, you're fully engaged in what you're doing, which helps you respond to situations thoughtfully rather than reactively. This practice can be particularly beneficial after leaving a narcissistic relationship, as it helps you regain control over your thoughts and emotions.

Mindfulness meditation offers various techniques to cultivate this state of awareness. One simple yet powerful method is breath awareness meditation. Sit comfortably, close your eyes, and focus on your breath. Notice the sensation of the air entering and leaving your nostrils. If your mind wanders, gently bring your focus back to your breath. This practice helps calm your mind and anchors you to the present. Another technique is loving-kindness meditation. In this practice, you silently repeat phrases of goodwill towards yourself and others, such as "May I be happy, may I be healthy, may I live with ease." Extend these wishes to loved ones, acquaintances, and even those you find challenging. This meditation fosters compassion and reduces feelings of resentment or anger. Body scan meditation involves focusing attention on different parts of your body, starting from your toes and moving up to your head. As you focus on each area, notice any tension or discomfort and consciously relax those muscles. This technique helps you become more aware of physical sensations and promotes relaxation.

Integrating mindfulness into daily life can significantly enhance emotional stability. Mindful eating practices involve paying full attention to the experience of eating. Notice the colors, textures, and flavors of your food. Chew slowly and savor each bite. This practice not only improves digestion but also enhances your appreciation for food. Mindful walking and movement are other ways to incorporate mindfulness into your routine. As you walk, focus on the sensation of your feet touching the ground. Notice the movement of your body and the rhythm of your breath. This practice can be calming and invigorating at the same time. Mindfulness can also be applied to daily routines like showering and cooking. When showering, feel the water on your skin, listen to the sound of the water, and inhale the steam. In cooking, engage all your senses—notice the ingredients' smells, colors, and textures. These practices turn mundane tasks into opportunities for mindfulness, making your day more peaceful and centered.

Maintaining a regular mindfulness practice can be supported by various apps and resources. Insight Timer offers a vast library of guided meditations, music tracks, and talks from mindfulness experts. It allows you to customize your meditation experience based on your needs and preferences. Headspace is another popular app that provides structured programs for mindfulness and meditation, making it easier to build a consistent practice. Many online and in-person mindfulness courses and workshops are available for those interested in more in-depth learning. These programs often include a combination of instruction, practice, and group discussions, providing a comprehensive understanding of mindfulness and its benefits.

By incorporating mindfulness practices into your daily life, you can cultivate a sense of calm and emotional stability. Whether through meditation, mindful activities, or using supportive resources, mindfulness offers a pathway to healing and resilience.

Journaling Prompts to Rebuild Self-Esteem

Journaling is a powerful tool for rebuilding self-esteem and processing emotions after leaving a narcissistic relationship. Writing provides a safe space to express your feelings, helping you gain clarity and perspective. When you journal, you can explore your thoughts and emotions without judgment, allowing you to understand your experiences better. This process of emotional expression can be incredibly therapeutic, helping you to release pent-up emotions and gain a sense of relief. Journaling also allows you to track your personal growth and progress over time. By regularly documenting your thoughts and experiences, you can see how far you've come and recognize your positive changes.

Daily affirmation prompts are a great way to focus on self-love and positive thinking. Start by listing three things you love about yourself. This can be anything from your kindness to your resilience. Writing down these affirmations helps reinforce positive self-perception and boosts your self-esteem. Another effective prompt is to write about a time you overcame a challenge. Reflecting on your past achievements reminds you of your strength and capability, reinforcing the belief that you can also handle future challenges. These daily affirmations serve as a constant reminder of your worth and help counteract the negative self-talk often instilled by a narcissistic partner.

Reflective journaling prompts encourage you to delve deeper into your past experiences and personal strengths. Describe a moment when you felt proud of yourself. This could be a personal accomplishment, a professional achievement, or a time when you stood up for yourself. Reflecting on these proud moments helps you reconnect with your inner strength and resilience. Another prompt is identifying the strengths that have helped you through difficult times. Acknowledge qualities like perseverance, empathy, or creativity. Recognizing these strengths reinforces your self-worth and empowers you to face future challenges confidently.

Gratitude journaling prompts foster a sense of positivity and appreciation for the good things in your life. Start by writing about three things you are grateful for today. These can be simple joys like a beautiful sunrise, a supportive friend, or a moment of peace. Focusing on gratitude shifts your attention away from negative thoughts and helps you appreciate the positives in your life. Another prompt is to describe a person who has positively impacted your life. Reflect on how their support and kindness have influenced you, and express gratitude for their presence. This practice of gratitude enhances your mood and strengthens your connections with others.

Engaging in these journaling practices can rebuild your self-esteem and healthily process your emotions. Emotional expression through journaling provides clarity and relief while tracking your personal growth helps you recognize your progress. Daily affirmation prompts reinforce positive self-perception, reflective prompts help you connect with your inner strength, and gratitude prompts foster a sense of positivity and appreciation. As you continue to journal, you will grow stronger, more confident, and more resilient.

Incorporating Yoga and Meditation into Your Routine

Yoga and meditation offer significant benefits for emotional healing and stress reduction. Practicing yoga regularly can improve your emotional regulation, helping you respond to stress and anxiety more calmly. Yoga poses, known as asanas, encourage you to focus on your breath and body, creating a sense of mindfulness that can alleviate emotional tension. This practice enhances both physical and mental well-being, promoting relaxation and reducing symptoms of anxiety and depression. Meditation complements yoga by providing mental clarity and fostering inner peace. Together, these practices create a holistic approach to healing, addressing both the mind and body.

Starting with basic yoga poses can help release emotional tension and foster a sense of calm. Child's Pose (Balasana) is a gentle, restorative pose that stretches the lower back and hips, promoting relaxation. To perform the Child's Pose, kneel on the floor, sit back on your heels, stretch your arms forward, and rest your forehead on the mat. This pose encourages deep breathing and a sense of surrender. Pigeon Pose (Eka Pada Rajakapotasana) is another effective pose for emotional release. It targets the hips, where many people store tension and stress. Begin kneeling, then slide one leg back and bring the opposite knee forward, positioning it near your wrist. Lower your torso over your front leg and stretch your arms forward. Hold this pose for several breaths, allowing the muscles to release tension. Heart-opening poses like Camel Pose (Ustrasana) can also be beneficial. Kneel with your knees hip-width apart, place your hands on your lower back, gently arch your back, and lift your chest towards the ceiling. This pose opens the heart and chest, encouraging a sense of openness and release.

Guided meditation practices can further enhance the benefits of yoga by promoting relaxation and emotional balance. Guided imagery for relaxation involves visualizing calming scenes or scenarios. Sit comfortably, close your eyes, and imagine a peaceful place like a beach or forest. Focus on the details—the sound of the waves, the smell of the trees, the warmth of the sun. This visualization can help reduce stress and promote a sense of tranquility. Chakra balancing meditation focuses on the body's energy centers or chakras. Sit comfortably and visualize each chakra, starting from the base of the spine and moving up to the crown of the head. Imagine each chakra glowing with vibrant energy, balancing and harmonizing your body's energy flow.

Progressive muscle relaxation involves tensing and then relaxing each muscle group in the body. Start from your toes and work your way up to your head, tensing each muscle group for a few seconds before releasing. This practice helps release physical tension and promotes relaxation.

Creating a consistent yoga and meditation routine is key to reaping the benefits of these practices. Start by setting a regular practice schedule. Choose a time of day that works best for you, whether morning, afternoon, or evening, and commit to practicing each day. Consistency is more important than duration, so even a short daily practice can be beneficial. Creating a dedicated practice space can also enhance your experience. Choose a quiet, comfortable area where you can practice without distractions. Decorate the space with items that promote relaxation, such as candles, plants, or calming artwork. Combining yoga and meditation sessions can create a holistic practice that addresses both physical and mental well-being. Start with a few minutes of meditation to center your mind, then move into your yoga practice. Finish with a longer meditation session or guided imagery to deepen your relaxation.

Incorporating yoga and meditation into your routine can provide a powerful foundation for emotional healing and stress reduction. These practices offer a holistic approach to well-being, addressing both the mind and body. Committing to regular practice can improve your emotional regulation, enhance your physical and mental well-being, and build resilience against stress and anxiety.

Success Stories of Emotional Recovery

Reading success stories can be a powerful source of inspiration and motivation. They validate your experiences, showing you're not alone in your struggles. These stories offer hope, demonstrating that recovery is possible and that others have walked the path you're on now. Seeing how others have overcome similar challenges can encourage you to continue your healing process, knowing there is light at the end of the tunnel.

Consider Sarah's story. After years of emotional abuse from her narcissistic partner, she felt lost and broken. Seeking therapy was her first step towards healing. In therapy, Sarah learned to identify and challenge the negative beliefs instilled by her ex. She also joined support groups where she met others who had faced similar struggles. Sharing her story and hearing others' experiences helped Sarah regain her self-esteem. She realized that her partner's cruel words did not define her worth. Over time, Sarah rebuilt her confidence, found new hobbies, and reconnected with friends and family. Her journey shows the power of therapy and community support in reclaiming one's life.

John's journey to finding peace involved mindfulness and meditation. Living with a narcissist had left him constantly on edge, filled with anxiety and self-doubt. He started practicing mindfulness to anchor himself in the present moment. Through breath awareness and loving-kindness meditation, John learned to let go of the past and focus on the present. Meditation helped him cultivate a sense of inner peace and resilience. He found that he could better manage his emotions and stay grounded by dedicating time each day to mindfulness. John's story highlights the transformative impact of mindfulness in healing from emotional trauma.

Emily's story is about achieving financial independence and emotional stability. Her narcissistic partner had controlled every aspect of their finances, leaving her feeling powerless. After their separation, Emily took control of her financial future. She educated herself about personal finance, set up a budget, and sought help from a financial advisor. Emily also focused on emotional healing, practicing self-care, and setting boundaries. She learned to say no and prioritize her well-being. Over time, Emily built a stable and fulfilling life for herself and her children. Her experience underscores the importance of financial independence and emotional self-care in recovery.

Survivors of narcissistic abuse share several key lessons that can guide your recovery. Setting boundaries is crucial. Establishing and maintaining firm boundaries protects your well-being and prevents further manipulation. Seeking professional help is another essential step. Therapists and counselors can provide the tools and support needed to navigate the complex emotions and trauma associated with narcissistic abuse. Practicing self-compassion and forgiveness is also vital. Be kind to yourself and allow yourself to heal at your own pace. Forgive yourself for any perceived mistakes and recognize that you did your best in a challenging situation.

Words of encouragement from others who have been where you are can be incredibly uplifting. One survivor shares, "You are stronger than you think." Another offers, "Healing is a journey, and you are not alone." These messages remind you that you possess the strength to overcome your challenges and that support is available.

Success stories and lessons from survivors emphasize the power of therapy, mindfulness, financial independence, and self-compassion. They show that recovery is possible and you have the strength to rebuild your life. As you continue your healing process, remember that you are not alone and that there is hope for a brighter future.

In the next chapter, we will explore strategies for co-parenting with a narcissist, focusing on setting boundaries and protecting your children's well-being.

Chapter Six

Co-Parenting with a Narcissist

When Amy first realized she had to co-parent with her narcissistic ex-husband, she felt a wave of dread. The man who had manipulated and controlled her for years was now going to be a permanent part of her and her children's lives. Amy knew setting firm boundaries was essential to protect her emotional well-being and ensure a stable environment for her children. This chapter dives into the importance of setting and maintaining these boundaries, offering practical advice to help you navigate this challenging terrain.

Setting Firm Boundaries with Your Ex

Setting firm boundaries is crucial when co-parenting with a narcissist. Narcissists thrive on manipulation and control, and without clear boundaries, they will exploit any opportunity to undermine your authority and emotional stability. Establishing boundaries helps prevent this manipulation, allowing you to maintain control over your life and decisions. It also protects your emotional well-being, creating a buffer between you and the narcissist's toxic behavior. Boundaries serve as a protective barrier, ensuring that your interactions remain focused on the children and do not devolve into personal attacks or emotional manipulation.

There are key areas where boundaries are essential. Communication methods and frequency should be strictly regulated. Narcissists often use communication as a tool for manipulation, bombarding you with messages or calls to maintain control. Limiting communication to necessary matters and setting specific times for discussions can help mitigate this. For example, all communication should be via email, which provides a written record and reduces the likelihood of impulsive, heated exchanges. Better still is to get a co-parenting app explicitly designed for high-conflict divorces. These apps can be beneficial in minimizing abusive communication, and most are admissible in court, should the need arise. Some of the most popular apps are: Our Family Wizard, coParenting, and AppClose, but many are available.

Visitation schedules and handovers are another critical area. Clearly defined schedules minimize the opportunities for the narcissist to disrupt your plans or create conflict. Ensure handovers are conducted in public places or with a third party, reducing the risk of confrontations. Decision-making processes regarding the children should also be clearly outlined. Joint decisions can be challenging with a narcissist, as they may use this as an opportunity to assert control. Establishing a process where decisions are made in writing or with the involvement of a mediator can help ensure that the children's best interests are always the priority.

Enforcing these boundaries requires consistency and determination. Written agreements and legal orders can provide a framework for maintaining these boundaries. For instance, a court-approved parenting plan can outline visitation schedules, communication methods, and decision-making processes, providing a legal foundation for your boundaries. Consistently adhering to established rules is crucial. Any deviation can be exploited by the narcissist, undermining your authority and the stability of the arrangements. If necessary, seek third-party mediation to resolve disputes and reinforce boundaries. Mediators can provide an impartial perspective and help facilitate constructive discussions, ensuring that boundaries are respected.

Handling boundary violations effectively is essential to maintaining control and stability. Documenting incidents of boundary violations is the first step. Keep a record of any breaches, noting the date, time, and nature of the violation. This documentation can be invaluable if you need to involve legal authorities or seek modifications to the parenting plan. Communicating consequences clearly is also important. Let the narcissist know that violations will not be tolerated, and outline the steps you will take if boundaries are breached. This might include seeking legal recourse or modifying visitation schedules.

Consider the case of Lisa, who successfully set firm boundaries with her narcissistic ex-husband. She limited communication to email, ensuring that all interactions were documented. Visitation handovers were conducted at a local coffee shop, with a friend present to witness the exchange. When her ex attempted to manipulate decisions regarding their children, Lisa insisted on written communication and involved a mediator when necessary. By documenting every violation and communicating clear consequences, Lisa maintained control and ensured a stable environment for her children. Her consistent enforcement of boundaries minimized the narcissist's ability to manipulate and control, allowing her to focus on her and her children's well-being.

By understanding the importance of setting firm boundaries and implementing strategies to enforce them, you can protect yourself from manipulation and ensure a stable, supportive environment for your children.

Communication Techniques to Minimize Conflict

Navigating communication with a narcissistic ex can feel like walking through a minefield. Keeping communication business-like and focused on the children is crucial to minimize conflict. This means avoiding personal topics that can trigger emotional responses. Stick to facts and logistics, such as school schedules, medical appointments, and extracurricular activities. Keeping the conversation centered on the children's needs reduces the opportunity for manipulation and control.

Using written communication can be particularly effective in minimizing conflict. Emails and text messages provide a written record of conversations, which can be invaluable if disputes arise. Written communication also allows you to take your time crafting responses, reducing the likelihood of impulsive, emotional reactions. Co-parenting apps like OurFamilyWizard offer additional benefits. These apps are designed to facilitate communication between co-parents, providing features like shared calendars, expense tracking, and secure messaging. The structured environment of these apps can help keep interactions civil and focused on the children.

Setting communication guidelines is another vital strategy. Establish specific times for communication, such as once a week or only during certain hours. This limits the frequency of interactions, reducing the chances of conflict. Clearly define what constitutes necessary communication. For example, stick to discussing the children's schedules, health, and well-being, and avoid bringing up past grievances or personal issues. Use neutral language and avoid emotional responses. Phrases like "I understand" and "Let's focus on what's best for the children" can help keep the conversation constructive and on track.

De-escalating conflicts during communication requires a calm and measured approach. If you feel yourself becoming emotional or angry, take time to cool down before responding. Step away from the conversation, take deep breaths, or engage in a calming activity. This pause allows you to regain composure and respond thoughtfully rather than react impulsively. Redirect conversations back to child-related topics if they start to veer into personal attacks or emotional territory. Assertively but calmly steer the discussion back to the matter at hand, emphasizing the importance of focusing on the children's needs.

Using "I" statements to express concerns without blaming can also help de-escalate conflicts. For example, instead of saying, "You never stick to the schedule," try, "I feel stressed when the schedule changes unexpectedly because it disrupts the children's routine." This approach focuses on your feelings and the impact on the children rather than accusing or blaming the narcissistic ex. It can reduce defensiveness and open the door to more constructive dialogue.

Following these five communication strategies will facilitate easier communication with your narcissist.

1. Establish specific times for communication.

2. Limit interactions to necessary matters only.

3. Use neutral language and avoid emotional responses.

4. Stick to discussing the children's needs and schedules.

5. Take time to cool down before responding to avoid impulsive reactions.

Implementing these communication techniques can create a more stable and less contentious co-parenting environment. Keeping interactions business-like, using written communication or a co-parenting app, setting clear guidelines, and employing de-escalation strategies can help you navigate the complexities of co-parenting with a narcissist while protecting your emotional well-being and focusing on the best interests of your children.

Protecting Your Children's Mental Health

Recognizing signs of emotional distress in your children is crucial when co-parenting with a narcissist. Children often express their struggles through changes in behavior or mood. You might notice your usually cheerful child becoming withdrawn or irritable. They might lose interest in activities they once enjoyed or exhibit sudden bursts of anger or sadness. Academic performance issues are another red flag. A drop in grades, difficulty concentrating, or a lack of interest in schoolwork can indicate your child is in emotional distress. Physical symptoms, such as headaches or stomachaches, are also common. These symptoms can be a child's way of expressing emotional pain when they don't have the words to articulate their feelings. Pay close attention to these signs and take them seriously.

Providing emotional support to your children is vital in helping them navigate the complexities of having a narcissistic parent. Maintaining open lines of communication is the first step. Encourage your children to talk about their feelings and experiences without fear of judgment. Let them know feeling confused, angry, or sad is okay. Validate their feelings by acknowledging their emotions and expressing empathy. Phrases like, "I understand that you're feeling upset, and it's okay to feel that way," can make a significant difference. Encouraging expression through creative outlets like drawing or writing can also be therapeutic. Art and journaling provide a safe space for children to express emotions they might find difficult to talk about. These activities can help them process their feelings and gain a sense of control.

Seeking professional help can provide additional support for your children's well-being. Child therapists or counselors are trained to help children navigate complex emotions and situations. They can offer coping strategies tailored to your child's needs and provide a safe space for them to express their feelings. Support groups for children of narcissistic parents can also be beneficial. These groups allow children to connect with others who share similar experiences, reducing feelings of isolation and providing a sense of community. Professional support can be instrumental in helping your children understand their emotions and develop healthy coping mechanisms.

Creating a safe and supportive home environment is essential for fostering emotional stability and security. Establishing consistent routines and rules provides a sense of predictability and safety. Regular meal and bedtimes and consistent rules and expectations can create a stable environment that helps children feel secure. Spending quality time together is equally important. Engage in activities your children enjoy, whether playing a game, reading together, or simply talking about their day. This dedicated time reinforces your bond and provides an opportunity for open communication. Encouraging healthy coping mechanisms like physical activity and hobbies can also support emotional well-being. Activities like sports, dance, or even regular walks can help release built-up tension and provide a positive outlet for stress.

Imagine a scenario where your child comes home from a visit with their narcissistic parent, visibly upset. They might be quieter than usual, reluctant to talk, or complain of a headache. Instead of dismissing these signs, you choose to address them. You sit down with your child, offering a comforting presence and an open ear. You encourage them to share their feelings, validating their emotions and offering reassurance. You suggest drawing or writing about their experience, allowing them to express their feelings. Recognizing the ongoing distress, you schedule an appointment with a child therapist who specializes in issues related to narcissistic parents. Meanwhile, you ensure that your home environment remains a safe haven, maintaining consistent routines and spending quality time together. By taking these steps, you address the immediate signs of distress and create a supportive framework that helps your child build resilience and emotional strength.

Documenting Interactions for Legal Purposes

When co-parenting with a narcissist, documenting interactions is crucial. This documentation serves multiple purposes, the foremost being to build a strong case in custody disputes. Courts rely heavily on evidence, and a well-documented history of interactions can reveal patterns of behavior that may influence custody decisions. Beyond that, thorough documentation protects you and your children from false accusations. Narcissists are skilled at twisting the truth, making it essential to have concrete records to counter their claims and accurately present your side of the story.

Documenting interactions involves several key components. Verbal and written communications should be meticulously recorded. This includes saving text messages, emails, and any other written exchanges.

These records can provide a clear picture of the narcissist's manipulative tactics, such as attempts to control or belittle you. Incidents of harassment or threats must also be documented. Whether these occur in person, over the phone, or through digital means, keeping a record of these incidents is vital. Note the nature of the harassment, any witnesses present, and how it impacted you and your children. If the police are involved in any incidents, follow up with the police department and get a copy of the police report.

Visitation exchanges and any issues that arise during these times are equally important to document. Document whether the narcissist adheres to the agreed-upon schedule or attempts to manipulate it. Note any comments or behaviors that indicate attempts to undermine your authority or disrupt your children's routine. These records can reveal a pattern of behavior that may be critical in custody hearings.

Practical methods for documenting interactions are essential to ensure accuracy and reliability. Keeping a detailed journal with dates and descriptions is a good starting point. Write down every interaction, including what was said, how it was said, and any significant details. This journal serves as a chronological record, making identifying patterns and presenting a coherent narrative in court easier. Doing this is an app that time stamps all entries, which can be especially helpful as it will hold more weight in court. Organizing emails and text messages in dedicated folders on your computer or phone is also beneficial. Label these folders by date or topic to ensure easy retrieval when needed.

Using co-parenting apps that provide documentation features can further streamline this process. Apps like OurFamilyWizard offer tools for tracking communication, sharing calendars, and documenting expenses. These apps often include features that prevent tampering, ensuring that records remain accurate and unaltered. The structured environment of these apps can also reduce the potential for conflict, as all communication is monitored and recorded.

Presenting documented evidence effectively in court requires careful organization and collaboration with your lawyer. Start by organizing your documentation chronologically. This allows the court to see the progression of events and behaviors. For each piece of evidence, provide context and explanations. Explain how the documented incidents impacted you and your children and why they are relevant to your case. Your lawyer can help compile this evidence into a coherent narrative, ensuring it effectively supports your arguments.

Working closely with your lawyer is crucial in this process. I cannot stress this enough: it goes back to why it was so important in the first place to hire an attorney with experience working with high-conflict divorces and narcissists. They can guide you on which pieces of evidence are most relevant and how to present them to the court. Regularly review your documentation with your lawyer, updating them on any new incidents or developments. This collaboration ensures that your case is well-prepared and that your evidence is presented in the most compelling manner.

The importance of documentation cannot be overstated. In custody disputes, where the stakes are incredibly high, having a well-documented history of interactions can make all the difference. It provides a clear, objective record that counters the narcissist's manipulations and supports your claims. By keeping detailed records of verbal and written communications, incidents of harassment, and visitation exchanges, you build a solid foundation for your case. Practical methods like maintaining a journal, organizing digital communications, and using co-parenting apps can streamline this process, ensuring that your documentation is accurate and comprehensive.

Creating a Stable Environment for Your Children

Establishing consistent routines is fundamental for providing your children with a sense of security and stability, especially when they are navigating the complexities of having a narcissistic parent. Regular meals and bedtimes create a predictable structure that children can rely on, fostering a sense of normalcy in their daily lives. Consistent rules and expectations are equally important. Children thrive in environments where boundaries are clear and consistent. This consistency helps them understand what is expected of them and reduces anxiety caused by unpredictability. By maintaining these routines and rules, you offer your children a stable foundation that counters the chaos often introduced by a narcissistic parent.

Creating a nurturing home environment goes beyond physical safety and encompasses emotional and psychological well-being. Providing a safe and comfortable living space is the first step. Ensure your home is a haven where your children feel secure and at ease. This can be achieved by creating cozy and personalized spaces for them to relax and unwind. Encouraging open communication and emotional expression is crucial. Let your children know their feelings are valid, and they can talk to you about anything. Foster a positive and supportive atmosphere by being attentive, empathetic, and encouraging. Celebrate their achievements, no matter how small, and provide comfort and reassurance during difficult times.

Promoting positive relationships with other family members and friends is another key aspect of creating a stable environment for your children. Encourage them to spend time with supportive relatives who can offer additional love and guidance. Arrange playdates and social activities to help them build friendships and social skills. Involving your children in community or extracurricular activities can give them a sense of belonging and purpose. These activities offer a healthy outlet for their energy and creativity and expose them to positive role models and peer groups. By fostering these connections, you help your children develop a robust support system that extends beyond the immediate family.

Balancing discipline and compassion in parenting is essential for creating a stable and nurturing environment. Setting clear and consistent boundaries is vital. Children need to know what is acceptable behavior and what is not. However, enforcing these boundaries with empathy and understanding is equally important. Use positive reinforcement and praise to encourage good behavior. Acknowledge their efforts and achievements, which helps build their self-esteem and confidence. When addressing behavioral issues, approach them with empathy. Understand the underlying reasons for their behavior and provide guidance on how to improve. Avoid harsh punishments that can lead to fear and resentment. Instead, focus on teaching and guiding your children toward better choices.

Consider Sarah, who successfully created a stable environment for her children after leaving her narcissistic ex-husband. She established a routine that included regular meals and bedtimes, which helped her children feel secure and grounded. Sarah made their home a safe, welcoming space filled with love and support. She encouraged her children to express their feelings openly and ensured they felt heard and understood. By fostering positive relationships with supportive relatives and friends, Sarah provided her children with a broader network of love and support. She balanced discipline with compassion, setting clear boundaries while using positive reinforcement to encourage good behavior. Her approach created a nurturing environment where her children could thrive despite the challenges posed by their narcissistic father.

Focusing on consistent routines, nurturing home environments, positive relationships, and balanced discipline can create a stable and supportive atmosphere for your children. This stability is crucial in helping them navigate the complexities of having a narcissistic parent and ensures they grow up in a loving, secure, and supportive environment.

In the next chapter, we will discuss the legal aspects of navigating the court system when divorcing a narcissist, including preparing for court appearances and presenting evidence effectively.

Chapter Seven

Rebuilding Your Support Network

When Karen finally decided to leave her narcissistic partner, she found herself facing an unexpected challenge: isolation. Over the years, her partner had systematically cut her off from friends and family. Karen felt alone and unsure how to reconnect with the people she once relied on. This chapter is for you if you are grappling with similar feelings. Rebuilding your support network is a crucial step in recovering from a narcissistic relationship and reclaiming your life.

Reconnecting with Isolated Friends and Family

Narcissists often isolate their partners from friends and family to maintain control. By severing your connections, they make you more reliant on them, reducing your sources of support and validation. This isolation can have significant emotional and social consequences. You may feel lonely, depressed, and disconnected from the world. Recognizing these signs in yourself is the first step toward rebuilding your support network. Reflect on your relationships and identify those that have been strained or lost due to your partner's influence.

Reaching out to loved ones after a period of isolation can be daunting, but it is essential. Start by drafting a heartfelt message or letter. Explain your situation honestly, acknowledging the time that has passed and expressing your desire to reconnect. You might say, "I know it's been a while since we last spoke, but I value our relationship and would love to reconnect." Setting up casual meet-ups or coffee dates can also help ease back into these relationships. These informal settings provide a comfortable environment to rebuild trust and understanding.

Being honest about your experiences and your need for support is crucial. Share what you have been through without placing blame. For example, you can say, "I've been in a difficult relationship that made it hard for me to stay in touch. I need support now more than ever." This honesty fosters empathy and encourages your friends and family to offer the support you need. Remember, the goal is to rebuild these connections, so approach these conversations with an open heart and a willingness to listen.

Addressing concerns and misunderstandings that may have arisen during your period of isolation is another critical step. Open and empathetic communication is key. Listen to their feelings and concerns and respond with empathy. Apologize for any hurt caused unintentionally. For instance, you might say, "I'm sorry if my absence hurt you. It was never my intention, and I hope we can move forward." Explain your situation without placing blame on anyone. This approach helps clear the air and paves the way for rebuilding trust.

Maintaining healthy boundaries with supportive friends and family is equally important. Identify your own needs and limits. Communicate these boundaries clearly and kindly. For example, you might say, "I need some time alone each week to recharge. I hope you understand." Ensuring mutual respect in all interactions helps maintain a healthy balance in your relationships. These boundaries protect your emotional well-being and prevent potential overstepping, even by well-meaning loved ones.

Take a moment to draft a heartfelt message or letter to a friend or family member you wish to reconnect with. Use this template to get started:

1. Greeting: Address the person warmly.

    ◦ Example: "Hi [Name],"

2. Acknowledge the Time Passed: Mention the time that has passed since you last connected.

    ◦ Example: "I know it's been a while since we last spoke."

3. Express Your Desire to Reconnect: Clearly state your intention to rebuild the relationship.

    ◦ Example: "I value our relationship and would love to reconnect."

4. Share Your Experience: Briefly explain your situation without placing blame.

    ◦ Example: "I've been in a difficult relationship that made it hard for me to stay in touch."

5. Ask for Support: Express your need for support.

    ◦ Example: "I need support now more than ever."

6. Suggest a Meet-Up: Propose a casual meet-up or coffee date.

- Example: "Can we catch up over coffee sometime soon?"

7. Closing: End with a warm closing statement.

- Example: "Looking forward to hearing from you. Take care."

This exercise helps you organize your thoughts and approach the conversation with clarity and sincerity. Reconnecting with loved ones is a vital step in rebuilding your support network and reclaiming your life from the influence of a narcissistic partner.

Finding and Participating in Support Groups

Joining a support group can be a lifeline for individuals recovering from the trauma of a narcissistic relationship. Support groups offer a unique blend of shared experiences and validation that can be incredibly healing. You immediately feel less alone when you walk into a room or join an online forum where people have faced similar struggles. The emotional support and understanding you receive from others who truly get what you're going through can be a balm for your wounded spirit. These groups also provide practical advice and coping strategies that others have tried and tested in similar situations. Hearing how others have navigated their challenges can offer you new perspectives and tools to handle your own.

Different types of support groups are available to meet various needs. In-person support groups offer the benefit of face-to-face interaction, which can be deeply comforting. These groups often meet in community centers, churches, or private homes. Online support groups and forums provide flexibility and accessibility, allowing you to connect with others from the comfort of your home. Specialized groups cater to specific demographics, such as single parents, LGBTQ+, or those dealing with co-parenting challenges. These specialized groups can offer tailored advice and a sense of community among people with similar backgrounds and experiences.

Finding the right support group may require effort, but the benefits are well worth it. Start by searching online directories and community listings. Websites that focus on mental health and abuse recovery often have directories of local and online support groups. Asking for recommendations from therapists or other survivors can also be helpful. They may know of reputable groups that are beneficial to others in similar situations. Once you have a few options, attend a few meetings to find the right fit. Each group has its own dynamic; finding one where you feel comfortable and supported is important.

Active participation in support groups can significantly enhance your experience. Share your story openly and honestly. This not only helps you process your own emotions but also allows others to connect with your experiences. Listening and offering support to others is equally important. Support groups thrive on mutual respect and understanding; your insights can be invaluable to someone else's healing process. Always respect the group's rules and confidentiality agreements. Trust is the cornerstone of these groups, and maintaining confidentiality ensures a safe space for everyone to share openly.

Checklist: Finding and Joining a Support Group

1. Search Online Directories: Look for listings on websites dedicated to mental health and abuse recovery.

2. Ask for Recommendations: Consult your therapist or fellow survivors for group suggestions.

3. Attend a Few Meetings: Test out several groups to find one where you feel comfortable.

4. Share Openly: Be honest about your experiences to foster connection.

5. Listen and Support: Offer empathy and advice to fellow members.

6. Respect Confidentiality: Follow the group's rules to maintain a safe space.

By taking these steps, you can find a support group that meets your needs and begin the process of healing and rebuilding your life.

Leveraging Online Communities for Support

Navigating the aftermath of a relationship with a narcissist can be isolating, but online communities offer a lifeline of support and connection. These platforms provide unique advantages that can be invaluable during your recovery process. One of the most significant benefits is accessibility and convenience. You can connect with others who understand your experiences from the comfort of your home, any time of day. This flexibility allows you to seek support whenever you need it without the constraints of meeting schedules or geographic limitations.

Anonymity and privacy are also crucial advantages of online communities. Many survivors of narcissistic abuse feel a deep sense of shame or fear of judgment. Online platforms often allow you to participate anonymously, giving you the freedom to share your story and seek advice without revealing your identity. This anonymity can make it easier to open up and be honest about your experiences. Additionally, online communities' diverse perspectives and experiences can provide a broader range of insights and coping strategies. Hearing from others who have navigated similar challenges can offer new ideas and approaches you may not have considered.

Several online platforms are particularly popular for those seeking support in recovering from narcissistic abuse. Facebook groups dedicated to narcissistic abuse recovery are a great place to start. These groups often have thousands of members, providing a wide range of perspectives and advice. Reddit forums like r/NarcissisticAbuse are another valuable resource. These forums allow for in-depth discussions and sharing of personal experiences in a supportive environment. Dedicated websites like Out of the Fog and PsychForums offer specialized forums and resources tailored to those dealing with personality disorders. These platforms can be an excellent source of information and support.

Engaging safely and effectively in online communities is crucial to ensuring your positive and beneficial experience. Protecting your privacy and personal information should be your top priority. Avoid sharing identifying details such as your full name, address, or workplace. Use a pseudonym if possible and adjust your privacy settings to limit who can see your posts and profile information. Recognizing and avoiding toxic or unhelpful interactions is also important. Not everyone online has good intentions, and some individuals may try to exploit your vulnerabilities. Trust your instincts and disengage from any interactions that make you feel uncomfortable or unsafe.

Reporting abusive or harmful behavior to moderators is another key aspect of engaging safely online. Most online communities have guidelines and rules to ensure a safe and supportive environment. If you encounter someone abusive, manipulative, or violating the community guidelines, report their behavior to the moderators. This helps maintain the integrity of the community and protects other members as well. Building a personal online support network can further enhance your experience. Connect with like-minded individuals who share similar experiences and values. Participate in live chats and virtual meetings to build deeper connections and gain real-time support. Sharing resources and advice with your online network can also be mutually beneficial, as you can learn from each other's experiences and strategies.

Resource List: Popular Online Platforms for Support

1. Facebook Groups: Search for groups dedicated to narcissistic abuse recovery.

2. Reddit Forums: Visit r/NarcissisticAbuse for discussions and support.

3. Dedicated Websites: Explore Out of the Fog and PsychForums for specialized forums and resources.

By leveraging the advantages of online communities, protecting your privacy, and building a personal support network, you can find the connection and support you need to navigate your recovery.

Building a Professional Support Team

When you find yourself navigating the complex aftermath of a relationship with a narcissist, assembling a professional support team can make an enormous difference. This team offers specialized knowledge and support, ensuring you are well-equipped to handle the legal, emotional, and financial challenges that lie ahead. A comprehensive support team typically includes therapists and counselors, legal advisors and lawyers, financial advisors, and medical professionals. Each of these experts plays a crucial role in helping you rebuild your life and regain your independence. The more support you have, the more unlikely you will be willing to give in to your abusive ex; your support groups will help you stay strong and stay the course.

Therapists and counselors provide the emotional support and therapeutic interventions needed to heal from the trauma of narcissistic abuse. They can help you process your experiences, develop coping strategies, and rebuild your self-esteem. Legal advisors and lawyers are indispensable when it comes to navigating the legal complexities of divorce and custody battles. They offer expert guidance on protecting your rights and interests, ensuring you have a strong case in court. Financial advisors assist in managing your finances, helping you achieve financial independence and stability. They can guide you through budgeting, investing, and planning for a secure future. Medical professionals, including your primary care doctor and any specialists you may need, ensure your physical health is taken care of, particularly if you have experienced stress-related health issues due to the relationship.

Finding qualified professionals who understand the dynamics of narcissistic abuse is crucial. Start by checking their credentials and experience. Look for therapists and counselors who specialize in trauma and abuse, legal advisors with experience in high-conflict divorces, and financial advisors with a track record of helping clients recover from financial manipulation. Ask for recommendations from trusted sources such as friends, family, and other survivors. Personal referrals can often lead you to professionals who have successfully helped others in similar situations.

Conducting interviews or consultations is an essential step in selecting the right professionals for your team. During these meetings, assess their understanding of narcissistic abuse and their approach to helping clients like you. For therapists and counselors inquire about their therapeutic methods and experience with trauma recovery. For legal advisors, ask about their strategies for handling high-conflict divorces and protecting clients' rights. Financial advisors should be questioned about their experience with budgeting, debt management, and long-term financial planning. These consultations provide an opportunity to gauge their empathy, communication style, and overall fit with your needs.

Coordinating care among different professionals is vital for ensuring comprehensive support. Share relevant information with your support team so they completely understand your situation. This might include legal documents, financial records, and medical reports. Scheduling regular check-ins and updates helps keep everyone on the same page and allows for adjustments to your support plan as needed. Ensure all professionals know your goals and needs, whether it's achieving financial stability, securing a favorable custody arrangement, or improving your mental health. This coordinated approach ensures that each aspect of your recovery is addressed holistically.

Evaluating and adjusting your support team is an ongoing process. Regularly assess your progress and satisfaction with the services provided. If you feel that a particular professional is not meeting your needs, be willing to seek feedback and recommendations for improvement. Sometimes, making changes to your support team is necessary to ensure you receive the best possible care. Don't hesitate to replace a professional if they are not providing the support you need. Your well-being is the priority, and having the right team is essential for your recovery.

Building a professional support team that understands the intricacies of narcissistic abuse is a crucial step in your healing process. By carefully selecting qualified professionals, coordinating their efforts, and regularly evaluating their effectiveness, you can ensure you have the comprehensive support needed to rebuild your life. This chapter has highlighted the importance of a multi-faceted approach to recovery, encompassing emotional, legal, and financial support. As you move forward, remember that each professional on your team plays a vital role in helping you reclaim your life and achieve a brighter future. The next chapter will delve into navigating the court system, providing you with the knowledge and strategies needed to succeed in family court.

Chapter Eight

Navigating the Court System

When Kelly entered the family courtroom for the first time, she felt a wave of anxiety wash over her. She had heard countless stories about the complexity of the legal process and the manipulative tactics her narcissistic ex-husband might employ. Kelly knew she needed to understand the inner workings of the family court system to navigate her divorce successfully. This chapter will explain the court system, giving you the knowledge and confidence to face the legal challenges ahead.

Understanding Family Court Procedures

The family court system is designed to handle legal issues related to family relationships, such as divorce, custody, and child support. Unlike criminal court, which deals with violations of law and criminal behavior, family court focuses on resolving disputes within the family structure. The primary goal is to ensure fair and just outcomes, prioritizing the well-being of all involved, particularly children.

In family court, judges play a pivotal role. They interpret and apply the law to the facts of your case, making decisions that affect your family's future. Clerks are responsible for maintaining court records, scheduling hearings, and assisting with administrative tasks. Other court personnel, such as bailiffs and court reporters, ensure proceedings run smoothly and are accurately documented. Understanding these roles can help you navigate the court process more effectively and know who to turn to for specific needs.

Divorce proceedings typically unfold in several key stages. The first stage is filing for divorce, where one spouse (the petitioner) submits a petition to the court, outlining the grounds for divorce and desired outcomes. The other spouse (the respondent) then has the opportunity to respond to the petition. This stage sets the foundation for the divorce process, and it's crucial to be thorough and accurate in your filings.

Next, temporary orders and hearings may be set to address immediate concerns, such as temporary custody arrangements, child support, and spousal support. These temporary orders provide stability and structure while the divorce is pending. The discovery process follows, where both parties exchange information and evidence relevant to the case. This stage involves gathering financial records, communication logs, and other documentation supporting your claims.

Mediation and settlement conferences often come next. These sessions aim to resolve disputes amicably, reducing the need for a contentious trial. A neutral third party, usually a mediator, facilitates discussions between you and your spouse, helping you reach agreements on property division and custody issues. Mediation can save time, money, and emotional stress if it is successful. However, if no agreement is reached, the case proceeds to trial. Given that you are divorcing a narcissist, you can expect your divorce case to proceed to trial.

Several common legal terms and concepts will arise during the divorce process. Legal custody refers to the right to make important decisions about your child's upbringing, such as education, healthcare, and religious instruction. On the other hand, physical custody pertains to where the child lives and the day-to-day care. Understanding the distinction between these terms is crucial when negotiating custody arrangements.

Contempt of court is another important concept. If your spouse violates a court order, such as refusing to provide documentation requested by the court, failing to pay child support, or not adhering to visitation schedules, they may be found in contempt of court. This can result in penalties, fines, or even jail time, depending on the severity of the violation. Temporary restraining orders (TROs) are also relevant. A TRO can be issued to protect one spouse from harassment or abuse by the other, providing immediate but short-term protection until a more permanent solution is established.

Jurisdiction and venue are critical factors in divorce cases. Jurisdiction refers to the authority of a court to hear and decide a case. In divorce proceedings, jurisdiction is typically based on residency requirements, meaning at least one spouse must reside in the state where the divorce is filed. Conversely, Venue refers to the specific location or court within the jurisdiction where the case will be heard. Choosing the appropriate venue is important, as it can impact the convenience and logistics of court appearances.

Determining the appropriate court for filing your divorce is a crucial step. Filing in the correct jurisdiction ensures that the court has the authority to make decisions in your case. Additionally, the venue can affect the court's familiarity with local laws and procedures, potentially influencing the outcome. Consulting with a knowledgeable attorney can help you navigate these decisions and ensure your case is filed correctly.

Understanding these aspects of the family court system gives you the knowledge needed to navigate your divorce effectively. By familiarizing yourself with the roles of court personnel, the stages of divorce proceedings, and key legal terms, you can approach your case with confidence and clarity. Remember, the goal is to achieve a fair and just outcome that prioritizes your well-being and that of your children.

Preparing for Court Appearances

Facing a court appearance can feel overwhelming, especially when dealing with a manipulative ex. Thorough preparation is crucial to reducing stress and anxiety. When you're well-prepared, you can present a clear and organized case, making it harder for your ex to manipulate the situation. Knowing what to expect and having all your documents in order can significantly ease your mind. One of the most effective ways to achieve this is by gathering all necessary documents well in advance. Financial statements, tax returns, communication records such as emails and text messages, and any evidence/documentation of abuse or manipulation, police reports, etc, are key. These documents form the backbone of your case and help substantiate your claims in court. I know I mentioned this earlier in the book, but I cannot emphasize this importance enough. These documents are your lifeline; be well-organized, thorough, and prepared.

Working closely with your lawyer is essential for effective preparation. Regular meetings and strategy sessions allow you to stay on top of your case and adapt to any new developments. Your lawyer can guide you on what to expect and help you develop a solid strategy. Mock hearings and role-playing exercises can be particularly beneficial. These sessions simulate the courtroom environment, allowing you to practice your responses and become more comfortable with the process. Discussing potential questions and responses with your lawyer helps you prepare for different scenarios, ensuring you're not caught off guard.

Personal preparation is just as important as legal preparation. How you present yourself in court can influence the judge's perception of your credibility. Dressing appropriately shows respect for the court and helps you feel more confident. Opt for professional attire that is conservative and understated. Practicing calm and confident body language is also crucial. Stand tall, make eye contact, and avoid fidgeting. These non-verbal cues convey confidence and reliability. Managing nerves through relaxation techniques can help you stay composed. Deep breathing exercises, visualization, and mindfulness can reduce anxiety and keep you focused.

One practical step is to create a checklist of documents and materials to gather in preparation for court. Financial statements and tax returns provide a clear picture of your financial situation, which is crucial for decisions related to alimony and child support. Communication records, including emails and text messages, offer concrete evidence of your interactions and can highlight patterns of abusive or manipulative behavior. Evidence of abuse or manipulation, such as photographs, medical records, police reports, or witness statements, is vital for substantiating your claims and protecting your interests.

Throughout this process, clear and open communication with your lawyer is paramount. Regular strategy sessions allow you to review and refine your case. Mock hearings and role-playing exercises prepare you for the courtroom environment, helping you anticipate and respond to various scenarios. Discussing potential questions and responses ensures you're ready for cross-examination and any surprises your ex might throw your way.

Personal preparation extends beyond just what you wear. Your demeanor and behavior in court are equally important. Dressing appropriately means opting for professional, conservative attire that shows respect for the court. Practicing calm and confident body language can significantly impact how you're perceived. Stand tall, make eye contact, and avoid fidgeting to convey confidence and reliability. Managing nerves through relaxation techniques is essential. Deep breathing, visualization, and mindfulness exercises can help reduce anxiety and keep you focused during the proceedings.

By focusing on thorough legal and personal preparation, you can navigate your court appearances with greater confidence and clarity. Being well-prepared reduces stress and anxiety and enhances your ability to present a clear and organized case. This comprehensive approach ensures you're ready to face the challenges ahead, empowering you to protect your interests and achieve the best possible outcome in court.

Presenting Evidence Effectively

When you enter the courtroom to present your case, the evidence you bring to the table will be your most powerful tool. Understanding the types of evidence that can be used in family court is crucial. Documentary evidence includes emails, text messages, and financial records. These documents can provide a clear, written record of interactions and transactions that support your claims. For example, emails, texts, and transcripts from apps and social media that show abusive language or text messages that detail threats can be compelling. Financial records, such as bank statements and tax returns, can demonstrate financial manipulation or hidden assets. Testimonial evidence comes from witness statements. Friends, family members, or professionals like therapists who have observed the dynamics of your relationship can provide valuable insights. Physical evidence, such as photos and videos, can also be powerful. Images of injuries, damaged property, or videos of confrontations can vividly illustrate the abuse or manipulation you have endured.

Organizing your evidence in a clear and logical manner is essential for effective presentation in court. Creating a detailed evidence binder is a practical first step. Use tabs and labels to categorize different types of evidence, such as financial documents, communication records, and witness statements. This organization allows you to quickly locate and reference specific evidence during the proceedings. Preparing a summary sheet for each piece of evidence can also be helpful. These summary sheets provide a brief overview of the evidence, including its relevance and key points. This helps you stay organized but also aids your lawyer in presenting a cohesive and compelling case. By methodically organizing your evidence, you ensure that everything is noticed and that you can present your case with clarity and precision.

When presenting evidence in court, it's important to introduce it through proper legal channels. Collaborating closely with your lawyer is crucial to ensure that each piece of evidence is presented effectively and follows legal protocols. Your lawyer can guide you in introducing evidence, whether through direct examination, cross-examination, or submitting documents to the court. Using visual aids and exhibits can also enhance your presentation. For instance, displaying charts that show financial discrepancies or projecting text messages on a screen can make your points more vivid and understandable to the judge.

These visual aids can help clarify complex information and make it easier for the court to grasp the significance of your evidence.

Anticipating and responding to objections from the opposing party is critical to presenting evidence. Common objections in family court include claims that evidence is irrelevant, hearsay, or improperly obtained. It's essential to be prepared for these challenges. Strategies for countering objections include demonstrating the relevance of the evidence to your case, showing that the evidence meets legal standards, and ensuring that all evidence was obtained legally. Consulting with your lawyer on potential challenges and objections can help you develop strategies to address them effectively. By anticipating objections and preparing thorough responses, you can strengthen your case and minimize disruptions during the proceedings.

Presenting evidence effectively requires a combination of thorough preparation, strategic organization, and clear presentation. By understanding the types of evidence, organizing it methodically, and anticipating objections, you can build a strong case that supports your claims and protects your interests. Throughout this process, close collaboration with your lawyer is essential to ensure that your evidence is presented in the most compelling and legally sound manner possible.

Handling Cross-Examination Tactics

Understanding cross-examination is crucial when preparing for your day in family court. Cross-examination serves a critical purpose: it tests the credibility of witnesses and the strength of their testimonies. During this process, the opposing counsel will ask you a series of questions to challenge your statements and cast doubt on your reliability. The typical structure starts with direct examination by your lawyer, where you present your narrative. This is followed by cross-examination, where the opposing lawyer attempts to poke holes in your story by asking you questions. Finally, your lawyer may conduct a redirect examination to clarify any points of confusion.

Opposing counsel often employs various tactics during cross-examination to unsettle you and undermine your testimony. One common tactic is asking leading questions designed to elicit specific responses that align with their narrative. These questions often contain the answer within them, making it difficult to provide a nuanced response. Another tactic involves highlighting inconsistencies in your testimony. The opposing lawyer may point out minor discrepancies in your statements, suggesting that your entire testimony is unreliable. Emotional provocation is another strategy; the lawyer may bring up sensitive topics or use a condescending tone to provoke an emotional reaction from you. This can make you appear irrational or overly emotional, weakening your credibility.

To effectively respond to cross-examination, it's vital to stay calm and composed under pressure. Maintaining your composure helps you think clearly and respond thoughtfully. When answering questions, be direct and succinct. Avoid rambling or providing unnecessary details that could be used against you. If a question confuses you or seems misleading, take your time to think before responding. It's perfectly acceptable to pause and collect your thoughts. You can also ask for clarification if a question is unclear. This shows that you are thoughtful and deliberate, qualities that judges respect.

Practicing for cross-examination with your lawyer is an invaluable part of your preparation. Role-playing cross-examination scenarios allow you to experience the pressure and intensity of the real thing in a controlled environment. Your lawyer can simulate the types of questions you might face and provide feedback on your responses. Reviewing potential questions and answers helps you anticipate the opposing counsel's tactics and prepare your responses. This preparation can significantly affect how effectively you handle the actual cross-examination. Developing strategies for staying focused and confident is also essential. Techniques like deep breathing, mindfulness, and visualization can help you remain composed and centered during the proceedings.

Consider the importance of not letting the opposing counsel rush you. They may try to speed up the questioning to catch you off guard. Instead, take your time to ensure your answers are accurate and considered. If you feel overwhelmed, it's okay to request a brief recess to regroup. This can help you maintain your focus and ensure your responses remain concise. Remember, your goal is to present your truth as clearly and accurately as possible.

Understanding the role and process of cross-examination, recognizing common tactics used by opposing counsel, and practicing your responses can equip you to handle this challenging part of the court proceedings effectively. By staying calm, direct, and prepared, you can maintain your credibility and strengthen your case, even under the intense scrutiny of cross-examination.

Post-Judgment Modifications and Enforcement

Understanding post-judgment modifications is vital for anyone navigating life after a divorce. Life is rarely static, and circumstances change, sometimes dramatically. These changes can necessitate adjustments to the original court orders regarding custody, support, or visitation. Post-judgment modifications are formal changes to these orders, reflecting new realities that weren't foreseeable during the initial proceedings. For example, if you or your ex-spouse experiences a significant change in income, you might need to modify child support payments. Similarly, if one parent relocates for a new job, visitation schedules may need to be adjusted to accommodate the new distances. Such modifications ensure that the court orders remain fair and relevant, taking into account the evolving needs and circumstances of all parties involved.

Filing for modifications involves several steps. First, gather evidence supporting the need for a modification. This could include financial records showing a change in income, medical records indicating a change in health, or documentation of a relocation. Once you have your evidence, the next step is to complete and submit the necessary forms to the court. These forms vary by jurisdiction, so it's crucial to consult your lawyer to ensure you're using the correct ones. After submitting the forms, you'll need to attend a modification hearing to present your case to the judge. Both parties can present evidence and argue for or against the proposed modifications during this hearing. The judge will then decide based on the evidence and arguments presented. This process can be daunting, but thorough preparation and legal guidance can make it more manageable.

Enforcing court orders is equally important. Despite the court's authority, some individuals may fail to comply with its decisions. Documenting any violations of court orders is the first step in enforcement. Keep detailed records of missed payments, denied visitations, or any other breaches of the court's directives. This documentation will be crucial if you need to file for contempt of court. Filing for contempt involves submitting a petition to the court detailing the violations and requesting enforcement. If the court finds your ex-spouse in contempt, they may face penalties, fines, or even jail time. Seeking enforcement through legal channels ensures that court orders are respected and that your rights, and those of your children, are protected.

Working with legal and support resources can make the process of post-judgment modifications and enforcement more manageable. Consulting with your lawyer on modification and enforcement strategies is crucial. Your lawyer can advise you on the best course of action, help you gather necessary evidence, and represent you in court. Seeking support from advocacy organizations can also be beneficial. These organizations often provide resources, support groups, and legal assistance to individuals navigating post-judgment issues. Utilizing mediation services for resolving disputes can offer a less adversarial modification approach. Mediation allows both parties to discuss their concerns and reach an agreement with the help of a neutral third party. This can be particularly useful for making adjustments to visitation schedules or custody arrangements without the need for a contentious court battle. In high-conflict cases, such as when dealing with a narcissist, this is unlikely to happen, so be prepared.

Understanding the necessity of post-judgment modifications and the steps involved in filing for them helps ensure that the court orders remain relevant and fair. Enforcing court orders and working with legal and support resources protects your rights and ensures compliance with the court's decisions. By staying informed and proactive, you can navigate post-judgment issues effectively, ensuring that the court orders serve the best interests of you and your children.

Chapter Nine

Handling Narcissistic Retaliation

When you finally decide to break free from a narcissistic partner, their reaction can be unpredictable and intense. One of the most common tactics they employ is hoovering—a term derived from the vacuum cleaner brand, symbolizing how narcissists attempt to suck their victims back into the relationship. Imagine you're finally feeling a sense of relief and newfound independence, only to be bombarded by unexpected messages, gifts, and apologies from your ex. These manipulative tactics aim to undermine your resolve and draw you back into their web of control.

Understanding Hoovering Tactics

Hoovering is a calculated strategy used by narcissists to regain control over their victims. It involves various manipulative behaviors designed to make you question your decision to leave. The narcissist may suddenly shower you with affection, offer tearful apologies, and promise to change their ways. These attempts are not born out of genuine remorse but are tactical moves to re-establish their dominance.

Recognizing common hoovering behaviors is crucial for protecting yourself. You might receive unexpected gifts or heartfelt messages that seem to come out of nowhere. The narcissist may feign illness or personal crises to evoke your sympathy, hoping you'll feel compelled to reach out and offer support. They might also revert to love-bombing—an intense barrage of flattery and declarations of love that initially drew you into the relationship.

The psychological impact of hoovering can be profound. These tactics create confusion and self-doubt, making you question your decision to leave. You might feel guilty, wondering if you were too harsh or should give them another chance. This emotional turmoil can undermine your resolve, making it difficult to maintain the boundaries you've set. The narcissist's goal is to destabilize your newfound independence and draw you back into a cycle of abuse.

To resist hoovering, it's essential to set and maintain strict boundaries. Clearly communicate that you do not wish to have any contact with them, and stick to this decision. Blocking their phone number, emails, and social media accounts can help prevent them from reaching you. If they persist, consider seeking legal measures such as restraining orders to protect yourself.

Ignoring attempts at contact is another effective strategy. When the narcissist realizes their efforts are futile, they may eventually give up. However, this requires an unwavering commitment to no contact. Engage in activities that promote your well-being and distract you from their attempts to re-enter your life. Surround yourself with supportive friends and family who can offer encouragement and remind you of why you left in the first place. You must stay strong and consistently resist their efforts of reconciliation.

Seeking support from professionals can also be invaluable. Therapists and counselors can provide strategies for coping with the emotional manipulation and help you rebuild your self-esteem. Support groups offer a sense of community and shared experiences, reinforcing that you are not alone in your struggle. Discussing your situation with those who understand the dynamics of narcissistic abuse can strengthen your resolve and provide practical advice for maintaining your boundaries.

By understanding the insidious nature of hoovering and implementing these strategies, you can safeguard your emotional well-being and continue moving forward on your path to recovery. Remember, the narcissist's attempts to regain control are not about love or remorse; they are about maintaining their dominance. Your strength and resilience are your best defenses against their manipulative tactics.

Countering Smear Campaigns

Imagine waking up one day to find that friends, family, and even colleagues have turned cold or distant. You soon discover that your narcissistic ex has been spreading false information about you, aiming to destroy your reputation and isolate you from your support network. This tactic, known as a smear campaign, is a common weapon used by narcissists to maintain control and protect their own image. By discrediting you, they shift the focus away from their own abusive behaviors, making you appear as the villain in the eyes of others.

A smear campaign involves the narcissist spreading lies and false rumors to damage your reputation. They might tell people that you were unfaithful, emotionally unstable, or even abusive. Their goal is to turn others against you, making it difficult for you to find support and validation. Narcissists are skilled manipulators and can be very convincing, often presenting themselves as the victim. This makes it even more challenging for you to defend yourself, as people may be more inclined to believe their seemingly sincere facade.

Recognizing the signs of a smear campaign is crucial. You might notice sudden negative behavior from mutual acquaintances who previously had no issues with you. False rumors and lies about your character or actions may start circulating within your social or professional circles. The narcissist may portray themselves as the victim, gaining sympathy and support from others while painting you as the antagonist. These tactics are designed to isolate you, making it harder for you to seek help and support.

The impact of a smear campaign can be devastating. Socially, you may find yourself isolated, losing friends and connections that were once a source of support. Your personal and professional reputation can be damaged, affecting your relationships and career opportunities. Emotionally, the constant barrage of lies can lead to significant distress and anxiety, making you question your self-worth and reality. The sense of isolation and betrayal can be overwhelming, leaving you feeling alone and vulnerable.

To counteract a smear campaign, it's essential to keep detailed records of interactions and evidence. Document any false claims, noting dates, times, and the context in which they were made. Save any written communications, such as emails or messages, that can provide evidence to refute the lies. By maintaining a thorough record, you can present factual evidence to counter the falsehoods being spread about you. Addressing false claims calmly and factually is another effective strategy. When confronted with lies, respond with clear, concise information that disproves the accusations. Avoid getting emotional or defensive, as this can play into the narcissist's hands and make you appear unstable. Stick to the facts and let your evidence speak for itself.

In some cases, seeking legal action for defamation may be necessary. If the smear campaign is causing significant harm to your reputation and well-being, consult with a lawyer to explore your options. Legal measures can provide a formal avenue to address the lies and hold the narcissist accountable for their actions. This can also serve as a deterrent, discouraging them from continuing their harmful behavior. Rebuilding your reputation through positive actions and transparency is another crucial step. Focus on demonstrating your true character through your actions and interactions. Engage in community activities, volunteer work, or professional endeavors that showcase your integrity and reliability. By consistently showing who you really are, you can begin to rebuild trust and mend relationships.

To stop the narcissist from wreaking havoc on your life with smear campaigns, you must follow these five strategies:

- Address False Claims: Respond calmly and factually to refute lies.

- Document False Claims Made against you by keeping a detailed record of interactions and accusations

- Seek Legal Action: Consult a lawyer if necessary to explore defamation options.

- Rebuild Reputation: Engage in positive actions and transparency to restore trust.

- Engage in Positive Activities: Volunteer, participate in community events, or contribute professionally.

By understanding the tactics used in smear campaigns and implementing these strategies, you can protect yourself from the narcissist's attempts to destroy your reputation. Remember, your true character will shine through, and those who matter will see the truth.

Dealing with Flying Monkeys

Flying monkeys are individuals who do the narcissist's bidding, often without fully understanding the extent of their manipulation. These people can be friends, family members, or even colleagues who the narcissist has skillfully manipulated to spread their narrative and attack you. They become unwitting pawns in the narcissist's game, carrying out tasks that further the narcissist's agenda and make your life more difficult. The term "flying monkeys" comes from *The Wizard of Oz*, where the Wicked Witch uses flying monkeys to do her dirty work. In this context, they serve a similarly destructive purpose.

Recognizing when someone is acting as a flying monkey can be challenging, but is crucial for protecting yourself. You may notice sudden involvement from mutual friends or family members who previously had little interest in your affairs. These individuals often repeat the narcissist's talking points almost verbatim, as if reading from a script. They might pressure you to reconcile or drop legal actions, claiming it's for the best or that you're overreacting. Understanding these behaviors can help you identify who has been co-opted into the narcissist's web and who remains a genuine ally.

The impact of dealing with flying monkeys can be emotionally and practically draining. Their involvement increases stress and conflict in your life, making it feel like you are constantly under siege. The feeling of being outnumbered and unsupported can be overwhelming, leading to a sense of isolation. This can complicate legal and custody battles, as flying monkeys might provide false testimonies or otherwise support the narcissist's claims. Their actions can create an environment where you feel like you are fighting a multi-front war, draining your emotional and mental resources.

Setting and enforcing boundaries is essential to managing interactions with flying monkeys. Clearly communicate your limits and the consequences of overstepping them. If a mutual friend or family member brings up the narcissist or tries to pressure you into actions that are not in your best interest, calmly but firmly state that you will not discuss the topic. Limiting or cutting off contact with flying monkeys is often necessary for your well-being. If someone repeatedly sides with the narcissist despite knowing the facts, it may be time to distance yourself from that person. Surround yourself with people who understand your situation and support your decisions.

Educating mutual acquaintances about the situation can also be beneficial. While you don't need to share every detail, providing a basic understanding of narcissistic behavior and manipulation can help others see through the narcissist's facade. This can turn potential flying monkeys into allies who support you rather than the narcissist.

It also helps disarm the narcissist's attempts to manipulate your social circle. Seek support from trusted individuals who understand the dynamics of narcissistic abuse. Whether it's a close friend, a therapist, or a support group, having a reliable support system can provide you with the emotional strength needed to deal with flying monkeys.

Remember, flying monkeys are often unaware of the full extent of the narcissist's manipulation. They may genuinely believe they are helping or doing the right thing. However, their actions can still be harmful. You can protect yourself from their influence by setting boundaries, limiting contact, educating others, and seeking support. It's important to stay focused on your well-being and not get drawn into the narcissist's manipulative games. Your mental and emotional health is paramount, and detaching from those who support the narcissist is a critical step in your recovery.

In dealing with flying monkeys, you may find it helpful to document any particularly manipulative or coercive interactions. Keeping a record can be valuable if you need to demonstrate a pattern of behavior in legal settings. Additionally, this documentation serves as a reminder of why you are taking steps to distance yourself from these individuals. It reinforces your decision to protect your well-being against the narcissist's far-reaching influence.

Maintaining No-Contact

After leaving a narcissistic partner, one of the most effective strategies for recovery is implementing the no-contact rule. This means cutting off all forms of communication with the narcissist. It involves blocking their phone numbers, emails, and social media accounts to ensure they cannot reach you. Additionally, it means avoiding places where the narcissist may be present, such as mutual friends' gatherings or familiar hangout spots. By doing so, you minimize the risk of accidental encounters that could trigger emotional reactions or attempts at manipulation.

There are several benefits to maintaining no-contact. Firstly, it significantly reduces emotional triggers and stress. Without constant reminders of the narcissist, you can begin to focus on your own well-being and healing. This space allows you to regain clarity and perspective, free from the fog of manipulation and control. Secondly, it provides the necessary time and space for healing. Emotional wounds need a safe environment to heal; no-contact creates that protective barrier. Lastly, it prevents further manipulation and abuse. By cutting off communication, you deny the narcissist the opportunity to continue their toxic behaviors, giving you the freedom to rebuild your life.

However, maintaining no-contact is not without its challenges. Emotional attachment and loneliness can make it incredibly tempting to reach out or respond to the narcissist. You might find yourself missing the good times and questioning if leaving was the right decision. Additionally, the narcissist's persistent attempts to reconnect can wear down your resolve. They may use various tactics, such as sending messages through mutual friends, showing up unexpectedly, or even faking emergencies to get your attention. External pressures from mutual friends or family members who do not fully understand the situation can complicate matters. These individuals might encourage you to reconcile or maintain contact, believing it to be the best course of action.

Creating a support system for accountability is crucial to stay committed to the no-contact rule. Surround yourself with friends, family, or support groups who understand your situation and can offer encouragement. They can help remind you of the reasons for maintaining no-contact and provide a listening ear when you feel tempted to break it. Engaging in activities that promote self-care and healing is another effective strategy. Focus on hobbies, exercise, therapy, or any activity that brings you joy and fulfillment. These activities not only distract you from thoughts of the narcissist but also contribute to your overall well-being.

Reminding yourself of the reasons for no-contact is essential for maintaining your resolve. Keep a journal where you document the negative experiences and manipulative behaviors you endured. Refer back to these entries whenever you feel the urge to reach out. This practice helps reinforce the reality of the situation, countering any romanticized memories that might surface. Preparing for potential attempts by the narcissist to break no-contact is also important. Have a plan for how you will respond if they try to contact you through new channels. This might include blocking new phone numbers, setting up email filters, or informing trusted friends not to relay messages.

By understanding the importance of no-contact and implementing these strategies, you empower yourself to break free from the cycle of abuse. Maintaining no-contact is a decisive step towards reclaiming your life, allowing you to focus on healing and create a future defined by your terms.

Legal Recourse for Harassment

Legal harassment is a deliberate pattern of behavior intended to intimidate, threaten, or otherwise disturb the victim. Unlike other forms of abuse that might be more emotional or psychological, legal harassment involves actions that can be addressed through the legal system. Repeated, unwanted contact, such as incessant phone calls, messages, or visits, falls under this category. Threats and intimidation, including any behavior that makes you feel unsafe or pressured, also qualify.

Additionally, stalking and surveillance, where the harasser monitors or follows you, can be grounds for legal action.

Recognizing signs of legal harassment is crucial for taking the appropriate steps to protect yourself. Persistent phone calls, messages, or uninvited visits are clear indicators. If you notice someone monitoring your movements or frequently appearing in places you visit, this constitutes stalking. Another sign is the harasser threatening legal action without basis, aiming to intimidate you into compliance. These behaviors are invasive and can escalate, making it essential to address them promptly.

Various legal options are available to counteract harassment. One of the most effective measures is filing for a restraining order or protective order. This legal document prohibits the harasser from contacting you or coming near you. It provides protection and legal recourse should the harasser violate its terms. Reporting harassment to law enforcement is another step. Police can document the harassment, provide immediate protection, and take action if the behavior continues. Seeking legal advice and representation is also crucial. A lawyer can guide you through the process, help gather evidence, and represent you in court if necessary.

To pursue legal recourse for harassment, follow these steps. First, document every instance of harassment. Keep a detailed log of unwanted contacts, threats, and any surveillance activities. Save all messages, emails, and voicemails as evidence. Next, consult with a lawyer who specializes in harassment or domestic abuse cases. They can provide tailored advice and help you understand your legal rights. Then, file a restraining order or protective order through your local court. Your lawyer can assist with the paperwork and ensure it is filed correctly. Once the order is in place, report any violations to law enforcement immediately. This ensures there is a legal record of ongoing harassment and can lead to further legal action against the harasser.

Navigating the legal system can be daunting, but taking these steps can provide you with the protection and peace of mind you need. Remember, you are not alone; resources and professionals are available to help you through this challenging time.

Chapter Ten

Overcoming Obstacles and Challenges

As you navigate the tumultuous waters of divorcing a narcissist, you may encounter numerous obstacles and challenges that test your resolve and resilience. One of the most insidious tactics a narcissist may employ is parental alienation. Imagine waking up one morning to find that your child, once loving and affectionate, has become distant and resentful toward you seemingly overnight. This sudden shift is not a coincidence but a calculated move by your ex to manipulate your child against you. Understanding and addressing parental alienation is crucial for maintaining a healthy relationship with your children and ensuring their well-being.

Coping with Parental Alienation

Parental alienation occurs when one parent deliberately tries to turn a child against the other parent. Narcissists use this tactic to maintain control and inflict emotional pain. They may manipulate the child's perception of events, paint themselves as the victim, and depict you as the villain. This behavior can be subtle, such as making negative comments about you in front of the child, or more overt, like fabricating stories of neglect or abuse.

Recognizing the signs and symptoms of parental alienation is the first step in addressing it. Your child may begin to exhibit unwarranted hostility toward you, refuse visitation, or parrot the narcissist's negative comments. They might also show an exaggerated loyalty to the alienating parent, even in the face of contrary evidence. These behaviors can be heart-wrenching to witness and may lead to a sense of helplessness and frustration. The psychological impact on children can be profound, leading to confusion, guilt, and emotional turmoil. They may struggle with identity issues as they are caught between the conflicting narratives of their parents.

Maintaining open lines of communication with your children to counteract parental alienation is essential. Encourage them to express their feelings and listen without judgment. Reinforcing positive memories and experiences can help remind them of your loving relationship. Avoid negative talk about the other parent, which can exacerbate the child's confusion and loyalty conflicts. Instead, focus on the positive aspects of your relationship with your child and demonstrate consistent, unconditional love.

Legal remedies are available to address parental alienation. Filing for custody evaluations can objectively assess the family dynamics and highlight any manipulation. Seeking court-ordered therapy for the children can help them process their feelings and receive professional support. Documenting instances of alienation, such as negative comments or refusal of visitation, can strengthen your case in court. Keep detailed records, including dates, times, and specific behaviors, to present a compelling argument to the judge.

Providing emotional support to your children during this challenging time is crucial for their well-being. Encourage them to express their feelings and validate their emotions. Involving child therapists or counselors can provide them with a safe space to explore their feelings and develop coping strategies. Creating a safe and nurturing home environment is essential. Establish consistent routines, offer emotional stability, and engage in activities that foster a sense of security and belonging.

Understanding parental alienation and implementing these strategies can help you maintain a healthy relationship with your children and protect their emotional well-being. As you navigate this challenging terrain, remember that you are not alone and that support is available to help you and your children heal and thrive.

Managing Emotional Exhaustion

Emotional exhaustion can creep up on you, especially when dealing with the relentless stress of a narcissistic relationship. It's not just about feeling tired; it's a profound, pervasive fatigue that affects every aspect of your life. You might feel constantly drained, struggling to muster the energy for even the simplest tasks. Concentration becomes challenging, making it difficult to focus on work or remember important details. Decision-making feels like an insurmountable hurdle, as your mind is clouded by overwhelming fatigue. You may also experience a profound sense of hopelessness, feeling as though nothing will change no matter what you do. This emotional exhaustion can make you feel trapped in a cycle of despair, unable to see a way out.

To combat this, prioritizing rest and sleep is crucial. Your body and mind need time to recover from the constant stress. Establish a regular sleep schedule, aiming for at least seven to eight hours each night. Create a calming bedtime routine to help signal to your body that it's time to wind down. This might include reading a book, taking a warm bath, or practicing gentle stretches. Avoid screens and stimulating activities before bed, as they can interfere with your ability to fall asleep. A well-rested body can better handle the demands of daily life and improve your overall resilience.

Engaging in regular physical activity is another powerful way to manage emotional exhaustion. Exercise releases endorphins, which are natural mood lifters. You don't need to commit to intense workouts; even moderate activities like walking, yoga, or dancing can make a significant difference. Find an activity you enjoy and incorporate it into your daily routine. Physical activity boosts your mood, helps reduce stress, and improves your sleep quality. It's an excellent way to channel your energy into something positive and constructive.

Practicing relaxation techniques can also alleviate emotional exhaustion. Techniques like mindfulness, meditation, and deep breathing exercises can help you calm your mind and reduce stress. Mindfulness involves focusing on the present moment without judgment, which can help you break the cycle of negative thoughts. Meditation can be as simple as sitting quietly and focusing on your breath for a few minutes daily. Deep breathing exercises, such as inhaling deeply through your nose and exhaling slowly through your mouth, can activate your body's relaxation response. These practices can help you cultivate a sense of inner peace and resilience.

Sometimes, managing emotional exhaustion requires professional help. Consulting with a therapist or counselor can give you the support and guidance you need to navigate this challenging time. A mental health professional can help you develop coping strategies, process your emotions, and work through the trauma of your relationship. They can also assess whether medication might be a helpful addition to your treatment plan. Medication can be particularly beneficial if you're experiencing symptoms of depression or anxiety that are interfering with your daily life. Don't hesitate to reach out for help; you deserve support.

Building a strong support system is another crucial step in managing emotional exhaustion. Reconnecting with friends and family can provide a network of people who care about you and want to help. Share your experiences with them, and let them know how they can support you. Joining support groups or community organizations can also be incredibly beneficial. These groups offer a sense of belonging and understanding as you connect with others who have faced similar challenges. Online peer support can be a great option if you prefer the anonymity and convenience of participating from home. These communities can provide valuable insights, encouragement, and a sense of solidarity.

The importance of taking care of and rebuilding yourself cannot be overstated. Take a moment to create a self-care plan tailored to your needs. This can be as simple as implementing some healthy habits. A good place to start is with your rest and sleep. Make sure you are on a regular sleep schedule, have a calming bedtime routine, and avoid screens before bed. Also, look at your physical activity and make sure you are participating in a physical activity you enjoy (walking, yoga, dancing) daily. Incorporating relaxation techniques such as practicing mindfulness or meditation daily will help you with the incredible amount of stress and anxiety you are dealing with. Seeking professional therapy, if needed, can be an enormous help in getting through your divorce and spending time with supportive friends and family.

By recognizing the signs of emotional exhaustion and implementing these self-care strategies, you can begin to alleviate the overwhelming fatigue and reclaim your energy and well-being.

Handling Smear Campaigns and Character Assassination

Smear campaigns are among the most destructive tactics a narcissist can employ. They spread false information and rumors about you to damage your reputation. Narcissists manipulate social and professional networks to isolate you and turn others against you. This manipulation often involves fabricating stories that paint you as the villain while they present themselves as the victim. Imagine waking up to see that people you once trusted are distant or hostile because they've been fed lies about you. Understanding how smear campaigns operate is crucial for protecting yourself and your reputation.

Protecting your reputation from a smear campaign requires a proactive approach. Start by documenting all false statements and accusations. Keep detailed records of any communication that contains lies or defamatory remarks. This documentation will be invaluable if you need to defend yourself legally. When necessary, issue clear and concise rebuttals to the false information. Address the lies directly, but avoid getting emotional or defensive. Stick to the facts and present your side calmly. In cases where the smear campaign causes significant harm, seek legal advice for defamation cases. Consulting with a lawyer can help you understand your options and take appropriate legal action.

Coping with the stress and anxiety caused by smear campaigns is equally important. Develop a thick skin, and don't take the attacks personally. Remember that the narcissist's behavior says more about them than it does about you. Focusing on your own truth and integrity helps you maintain your self-worth and confidence. Practicing mindfulness and self-compassion can also be beneficial. Mindfulness involves staying present and not letting negative thoughts take over. Self-compassion means treating yourself with the same kindness and understanding that you would offer a friend. These practices can help you stay grounded and resilient in the face of attacks.

Rebuilding trust and credibility with your social and professional circles is a gradual process, but it can be done. Maintain transparency and honesty in all your interactions. Being open about your experiences without oversharing can help others see your side of the story. Engaging in positive community activities can also help restore your reputation. Volunteer work, community involvement, or professional contributions showcase your integrity and dedication. Seeking character references from trusted individuals can further bolster your credibility. These references provide third-party validation of your character, countering the lies the narcissist spreads.

Understanding smear campaigns and taking steps to protect your reputation can help you navigate this challenging aspect of dealing with a narcissist. Remember, the truth will eventually come to light, and your integrity will shine through.

Counteracting Financial Manipulation

Financial manipulation is a common tactic used by narcissists to maintain control and create dependency. You may find that your narcissistic partner controls access to joint accounts, making it nearly impossible for you to access funds without their approval. This tactic ensures that you remain financially dependent on them, limiting your options and making it harder to leave. They might also hide or misappropriate assets, moving money into secret accounts or making substantial purchases without your knowledge. These actions can leave you in the dark about your financial situation and make you vulnerable to financial abuse. Creating unnecessary financial dependencies is another strategy; perhaps they've insisted you quit your job to focus on the household, leaving you without an independent income source. These manipulative behaviors are designed to strip you of financial autonomy and keep you trapped in the relationship.

Regaining financial control is a critical step towards independence. Start by opening individual bank accounts to separate your finances from your ex's. This move ensures that any income you earn is under your control and not accessible to them. Tracking and documenting all financial transactions is also essential. Keep records of joint account statements, receipts, and any financial communications. This documentation will be invaluable if you need to present evidence of financial manipulation in court. Seeking financial independence through employment or education can provide you with the resources you need to support yourself. If you've been out of the workforce, consider taking courses or certifications to update your skills. Employment provides financial stability and boosts your self-esteem and sense of autonomy.

Legal protections are available to counteract financial abuse. Filing for temporary financial orders can provide immediate relief by ensuring you have access to necessary funds during the divorce proceedings. These orders can mandate that your ex provide financial support or freeze joint accounts to prevent further manipulation. Seeking court intervention for asset protection is another option. The court can issue orders to protect joint assets, ensuring they are not sold or hidden during the divorce process. Consulting with a financial advisor or attorney specializing in high-conflict divorces can offer expert advice and strategies tailored to your situation. These professionals can help you navigate complex financial landscapes, protecting your rights and interests.

Building financial literacy is a vital component of regaining control and confidence. Taking financial management courses can provide you with the knowledge and skills needed to manage your finances effectively. Many community colleges and online platforms offer courses on budgeting, investing, and financial planning. Reading books and resources on personal finance can also be incredibly beneficial. Titles like "Your Money or Your Life" by Vicki Robin and Joe Dominguez or "The Total Money Makeover" by Dave Ramsey offer practical advice and strategies for financial independence. Using budgeting tools and apps to track spending and savings can help you stay on top of your finances. Apps like Mint, YNAB (You Need a Budget), and PocketGuard provide user-friendly interfaces for tracking income, expenses, and savings goals. These tools can help you create a budget, monitor your spending, and ensure you're on track to meet your financial goals.

Resource List: Building Financial Literacy

1. Financial Management Courses: Look for courses at community colleges or online platforms like Coursera and Udemy.

2. Books on Personal Finance: Consider reading "Your Money or Your Life" by Vicki Robin and Joe Dominguez or "The Total Money Makeover" by Dave Ramsey.

3. Budgeting Tools and Apps: Use apps like Mint, YNAB (You Need a Budget), and PocketGuard to track spending and savings.

By taking these steps to counteract financial manipulation, you can regain control over your finances and build a stable, independent future. This journey requires determination and resilience, but with the right tools and support, you can achieve financial independence and protect yourself from further abuse.

Chapter Eleven

Embracing a New Beginning

Maria stood in front of her easel, brush in hand, feeling a rush of emotions she hadn't experienced in years. Painting had always been her sanctuary, a place where she could lose herself in colors and shapes. But during her marriage to a narcissist, she had abandoned this passion. Her ex-husband's constant criticism and manipulation had eroded her self-worth, making her feel unworthy of even her own hobbies. Now, as she dipped her brush into vibrant paint, she felt a spark of her old self returning. This chapter is dedicated to helping you reclaim your identity and self-worth, just as Maria is beginning to do.

Reclaiming Your Identity and Self-Worth

Understanding the impact of narcissistic abuse on your identity is the first step in rebuilding yourself. Narcissists thrive on control, and they often achieve this by constantly criticizing and manipulating their partners. Over time, this relentless assault on your self-esteem can make you question your own worth. You may have heard phrases like, "You're too sensitive," or, "No one else would put up with you," so many times that they start to feel true. This constant criticism not only chips away at your confidence but also isolates you from sources of validation and support. As a result, you may have lost touch with who you are and what you love.

One of the most devastating effects of narcissistic abuse is the loss of personal interests and passions. Activities that once brought you joy and fulfillment may have been dismissed as trivial or selfish by your narcissistic partner. You might have given them up to avoid conflict or to meet the endless demands placed upon you. Rediscovering these interests can be a powerful way to reclaim your identity. Start by making a list of activities and hobbies you once enjoyed. Ask yourself what used to make you feel alive and connected to your true self. Then, make a conscious effort to reintroduce these activities into your life, even if it's just for a few minutes a day.

Building self-confidence after narcissistic abuse can feel like an uphill battle, but it's entirely possible with small, achievable steps. Begin by setting realistic, short-term goals and celebrating each success, no matter how minor it may seem. These small victories will help you rebuild a sense of accomplishment and self-worth. Practicing positive self-affirmations daily can also be transformative. Write down affirmations like, "I am worthy of love and respect," and repeat them to yourself each morning. Seek feedback and encouragement from trusted friends and family who see and appreciate your true value. Their support can provide a much-needed counterbalance to the negative messages you've internalized.

Therapeutic techniques can also play a crucial role in reclaiming your identity. Identity-focused journaling exercises can help you explore and express your true self. Write about who you were before the relationship, who you are now, and who you want to become. Visualization exercises can be particularly effective. Close your eyes and imagine the future self you aspire to be. What does this person look like? What do they do? How do they feel? Art therapy is another valuable tool. It allows you to express and explore your identity through creative means, providing a tangible representation of your inner world.

Reflection Section: Identity-Focused Journaling Exercise

Take some time to reflect on the following prompts in your journal:

1. Who was I before this relationship?

2. What activities and hobbies used to bring me joy?

3. How did my partner's criticism and manipulation affect my self-worth?

4. Who do I want to become moving forward?

5. What small steps can I take today to reconnect with my true self?

By engaging with these exercises and techniques, you can begin to rebuild your self-confidence and reconnect with the passions that define you. Remember, reclaiming your identity is not a destination but a continuous process of self-discovery and growth. As you move forward, celebrate each small victory and embrace the journey of rediscovering your true self.

Setting Goals for Your New Life

Setting goals is a powerful way to create a fulfilling and purposeful life after leaving a narcissistic relationship. When you set goals, you provide yourself with a clear direction and a sense of purpose. It helps transform vague desires into concrete steps and offers a roadmap to follow. This process can be incredibly empowering, especially when you need to measure your progress and celebrate your achievements. Knowing where you want to go and how you plan to get there can make all the difference in your journey to recovery and growth.

Start by distinguishing between short-term and long-term goals. Short-term goals are daily or weekly tasks that are manageable and immediately actionable. These could be as simple as committing to a daily walk for your well-being or setting aside time each week to reconnect with a hobby you once loved. Long-term goals, on the other hand, relate to broader aspirations such as career advancement or personal development. These might involve pursuing further education, changing careers, or achieving significant personal milestones. It's vital to balance both types of goals to maintain motivation and see tangible progress while working towards more significant achievements.

A practical approach to goal setting is the SMART framework. SMART stands for Specific, Measurable, Achievable, Relevant, and Time-bound. For instance, instead of setting a vague goal like "I want to get fit," a SMART goal would be "I will walk 30 minutes every morning for the next three months." This goal is specific (walking for 30 minutes), measurable (you can track the time), achievable (a reasonable daily task), relevant (improves fitness), and time-bound (three months). By breaking down your aspirations into SMART goals, you create a clear, actionable plan that increases your chances of success.

Creating a vision board can be a fun and inspiring way to visualize your goals and dreams. Start by collecting images, words, and phrases that resonate with your aspirations. These could be cutouts from magazines, printed images from the internet, or even personal photographs. Assemble these elements on a board, arranging them in a way that feels meaningful to you. Place your vision board somewhere visible, like your bedroom or workspace, so you can see it daily. This visual reminder keeps your goals at the forefront of your mind, motivating you to take consistent action toward achieving them.

Exercise: Creating Your Vision Board

Gather materials like magazines, scissors, glue, and a large board or poster. Spend time identifying images and words that represent your goals. Arrange these elements on the board in an inspiring way. Place your vision board in a spot where you'll see it every day.

Setting goals and visualizing them through a vision board can transform your aspirations into reality. Setting short-term and long-term goals, using the SMART framework, and creating a vision board will pave the way for a purposeful and fulfilling life. Each step you take brings you closer to reclaiming your identity and building the life you deserve.

Fostering New Relationships and Friendships

Forming healthy, supportive relationships after leaving a narcissistic partner is crucial for your emotional well-being. The first step is recognizing red flags and ensuring mutual respect in any new connection. Trust your instincts; if someone exhibits controlling behavior, excessive neediness, or a lack of empathy, these are signs to proceed with caution. Mutual respect is foundational. Establish and respect boundaries early on, discussing your needs and limits openly. If someone dismisses or disregards your boundaries, it's a clear indication that this relationship may not be healthy for you.

Making new friends can feel daunting, especially if you've been isolated for a long time. Start by joining clubs, groups, or classes that align with your interests. This gives you a chance to meet like-minded individuals and helps you reconnect with your passions. Community activities and volunteering are excellent ways to expand your social circle while contributing to a cause you care about. Both settings provide natural opportunities for social interaction, making it easier to form genuine connections.

Dating again after narcissistic abuse comes with its own set of challenges. It's important to take time to heal before entering new relationships. Rushing into dating can lead to repeating old patterns. When you feel ready, communicate openly and honestly with potential partners about your past experiences and current needs. This transparency can foster trust and understanding. Be mindful to avoid falling into the same traps that characterized your previous relationship. Recognize unhealthy dynamics early and prioritize your emotional health above all else.

Strengthening existing relationships can provide a solid support network. Regular communication and check-ins with friends and family help maintain these bonds. Make an effort to plan activities and outings together. Whether it's a weekly coffee date, a hike, or a simple phone call, these interactions remind both you and your loved ones of the importance of your connection. Rebuilding trust and intimacy takes time, but with consistent effort, you can restore and even enhance these relationships.

Celebrating Small Wins and Progress

Recognizing and celebrating small wins is a powerful way to maintain motivation and positivity as you navigate your new life. The process of recovering from a narcissistic relationship can be long and challenging, so it's vital to acknowledge your progress along the way. Celebrating small victories reinforces positive behavior and growth. It provides a sense of accomplishment and joy, which can be particularly uplifting during difficult times. When you take the time to celebrate these milestones, you not only validate your efforts but also build momentum for future successes. This practice helps you stay focused and motivated, even when the road ahead seems daunting.

There are many ways to celebrate milestones and achievements. Treating yourself to a favorite activity or item can be a delightful reward. Whether it's watching a movie, enjoying a spa day, or buying that book you've been eyeing, these treats can serve as tangible reminders of your progress. Sharing your successes with friends and family can also be incredibly rewarding. When you let loved ones in on your achievements, you receive their support and encouragement and strengthen your bond with them. Another creative way to celebrate is by creating a "victory jar." Each time you achieve a goal, write it down on a small piece of paper and place it in the jar. Over time, you'll have a collection of accomplishments to look back on, reminding you of how far you've come.

Tracking your progress is crucial for maintaining a sense of direction and purpose. Keeping a journal of daily accomplishments allows you to see your growth in real time. Each entry, no matter how small, is a step forward. Using apps or planners to track goals and milestones can also be highly effective. These tools offer structured ways to monitor your progress, set reminders, and celebrate achievements.

By consistently tracking your progress, you create a tangible record of your journey, making it easier to stay motivated and focused.

Another important practice is regularly reflecting on your achievements. Monthly reflection sessions can be a great way to review your progress and set new goals. Take time at the end of each month to reflect on what you've accomplished. Write letters to yourself acknowledging your progress and expressing pride in your achievements. These letters can serve as powerful reminders of your resilience and determination. By regularly reflecting on your achievements, you reinforce your sense of self-worth and build confidence in your ability to overcome challenges.

Exercise: Creating a "Victory Jar"

To create a "victory jar," find a jar or container that you like. Each time you achieve a goal, write it down on a small piece of paper. Include the date and a brief description of the achievement. Fold the paper and place it in the jar. Over time, this jar will fill with notes of your accomplishments, serving as a tangible reminder of your progress. When you're feeling down or unmotivated, open the jar and read through your achievements. This practice can provide a significant boost to your morale and motivation.

Celebrating small wins and tracking your progress can make a considerable difference in your recovery and growth. By acknowledging your efforts and reflecting on your achievements, you build a strong foundation for continued success.

Long-Term Strategies for Emotional and Financial Well-Being

Developing emotional resilience after leaving a narcissistic relationship is a continuous process that requires dedication and self-compassion. Continuing therapy or counseling is crucial. Regular sessions with a skilled therapist can provide a safe space to explore your feelings, develop coping strategies, and work through any lingering trauma. Therapy is not just for crisis moments; it's a long-term investment in your mental health. Alongside professional help, engage in regular self-care routines that nourish both body and mind. Whether it's daily meditation, exercise, or simply taking time to relax with a good book, these small acts of self-care can significantly bolster your emotional resilience.

Building a network of supportive relationships is equally important. Surround yourself with people who uplift and encourage you. These could be friends, family, or members of support groups who understand your experiences and can offer empathy and advice. Regularly connecting with these individuals can provide a sense of belonging and security, which is vital for emotional well-being. Remember that it's okay to lean on others. Accepting support is a sign of strength, not weakness. By fostering these supportive relationships, you create a safety net that can help you navigate the ups and downs of life with greater resilience.

Financial stability is another cornerstone of long-term well-being. Regularly reviewing and adjusting your budget ensures that you stay on top of your finances and can make informed decisions. Set aside time each month to go over your income, expenses, and savings goals. This habit helps you manage your money more effectively and reduces financial stress. Investing in long-term savings and retirement plans is also crucial. Whether it's contributing to a 401(k), an IRA, or setting up an emergency fund, these investments provide financial security and peace of mind.

Seeking financial education and resources can empower you to make better financial decisions. Take advantage of online courses, workshops, and books on personal finance. The more you know, the better equipped you'll be to handle financial challenges and opportunities. Financial literacy is a lifelong journey; continually educating yourself can lead to greater financial independence and confidence.

Personal development is an ongoing process that enriches your life and opens up new opportunities. Taking courses or workshops to learn new skills can be incredibly rewarding. Whether it's a cooking class, a coding boot camp, or a public speaking workshop, these experiences broaden your horizons and boost your confidence. Set personal development goals, such as reading a certain number of books per year or learning a new language. These goals keep you motivated and give you a sense of accomplishment. Exploring new career opportunities or advancing in your current career can also be a significant part of your personal development journey. Seek out professional development opportunities, network with industry peers, and stay updated on trends in your field.

Maintaining a positive mindset is essential for long-term well-being. Practicing gratitude and mindfulness daily can help you stay grounded and focused on the positives in your life. Start each day by reflecting on what you're grateful for, no matter how small. This simple practice can shift your perspective and improve your overall mood. Surround yourself with positive influences, whether it's through uplifting books, motivational podcasts, or spending time with optimistic people. Setting aside time for hobbies and activities that bring you joy is equally important. Whether it's painting, hiking, or playing a musical instrument, these activities provide a creative outlet and a break from daily stressors.

By focusing on these long-term strategies for emotional and financial well-being, you can build a fulfilling and resilient life, rich with opportunities for growth and happiness.

Moving Forward with Confidence and Hope

Embracing change and being open to new opportunities can feel daunting, especially after leaving a relationship with a narcissist. However, viewing change as a chance for growth and learning can transform your outlook. Each new experience becomes an opportunity to discover more about yourself and what you truly want from life. Stepping out of your comfort zone is essential in this process. It might be intimidating at first, but trying new activities, meeting new people, and exploring different interests can lead to unexpected and fulfilling experiences. Embrace the unknown as a path to personal growth and self-discovery.

Setting a positive tone for the future involves more than just wishful thinking. It starts with visualizing a fulfilling and happy future. Picture the life you want to lead, the person you want to become, and the experiences you wish to have. This vision can serve as a guiding star, helping you stay focused on your goals. Creating a personal manifesto or vision statement can also be a powerful tool. Write down your core values, aspirations, and the principles you want to live by. This document serves as a constant reminder of your commitments to yourself and your future, helping you stay on track even when challenges arise.

Staying connected with support networks is crucial for ongoing encouragement and growth. Regularly attending support group meetings can provide a sense of community and shared understanding. These gatherings offer a safe space to express your feelings, share experiences, and receive advice from others who have been in similar situations. Keeping in touch with supportive friends and family is equally important. They can offer a listening ear, words of encouragement, and practical help when needed. These connections remind you that you are not alone and that there are people who care about your well-being and want to see you succeed.

One of the most important aspects of moving forward is fostering self-compassion and patience with yourself. Recognize that setbacks are a natural part of growth and do not define your journey. When you encounter obstacles, remind yourself that they are opportunities to learn and become stronger. Be kind and forgiving to yourself, just as you would be to a close friend. Practice self-compassion by acknowledging your efforts and celebrating your progress, no matter how small. Patience is key; healing and growth take time, and giving yourself the grace to move at your own pace is important.

By embracing change, setting a positive tone for the future, staying connected with support networks, and fostering self-compassion, you can move forward with confidence and hope. These strategies will help you build a fulfilling and resilient life, rich with opportunities for growth and happiness.

Conclusion

As you reach the end of this book, I want to acknowledge the courage it takes to embark on such a challenging journey. The purpose of this book was to prepare you for the high-conflict process of divorcing a narcissist and to empower you to rebuild your life. You have learned about the legal strategies, emotional resilience, and practical steps necessary to navigate this tumultuous time.

Throughout our chapters, we have covered a wide range of topics, each designed to equip you with the knowledge and tools you need. We began by understanding Narcissistic Personality Disorder (NPD), recognizing the traits and behaviors that define a narcissist. This foundational knowledge is crucial in helping you identify the manipulation and control tactics that may have been part of your relationship.

We then moved on to preparing for the legal battle, discussing the importance of gathering evidence, choosing the right lawyer, and documenting interactions. We explored how to create a safety plan to protect yourself and your children, focusing on securing important documents, finding safe housing, and establishing emergency contacts. Financial independence and recovery were also key topics, with strategies for regaining control of your finances, budgeting, and planning for a secure future.

Emotional healing and self-care were emphasized, with therapeutic exercises, mindfulness practices, and journaling prompts to help you rebuild your self-esteem. We discussed the challenges of co-parenting with a narcissist, setting firm boundaries, and protecting your children's mental health. Rebuilding your support network, navigating the court system, and handling narcissistic retaliation were covered in detail to ensure you are well-prepared for any obstacles that may arise.

Key takeaways from this book include the importance of understanding NPD and recognizing the signs of emotional abuse. Gathering and documenting evidence is crucial for legal success, while creating a safety plan ensures your physical and emotional well-being. Financial independence is achievable through careful planning and budgeting, and emotional healing requires self-care and professional support. Setting firm boundaries and protecting your children's mental health are essential when co-parenting, and rebuilding your support network is vital for long-term recovery.

As you move forward, remember that you possess incredible strength and resilience. You have already taken the first steps towards a better future by seeking knowledge and support. It is normal to feel overwhelmed, but every small step you take is a victory. Celebrate your progress, no matter how small, and give yourself credit for the strides you have made.

I encourage you to take proactive steps towards your healing and legal journey. Reach out to trusted friends and family, join support groups, and seek professional help when needed. Continue to educate yourself about narcissistic abuse and recovery, and never hesitate to ask for help. Your well-being and happiness are worth fighting for, and you deserve a life free from manipulation and control.

For continued support and education, consider exploring the following resources:

- "The Body Keeps the Score" by Bessel van der Kolk
- "Why Does He Do That?" by Lundy Bancroft
- Online communities such as Reddit's r/NarcissisticAbuse
- Support organizations like the National Domestic Violence Hotline
- Financial planning tools and apps like Mint and YNAB

As we conclude, I want to leave you with words of hope and positivity. You are not defined by your past or the abuse you have endured. You have the power to create a new beginning, one filled with joy, peace, and fulfillment. Embrace this journey with an open heart and a determined spirit. You are stronger than you realize, and your future is bright.

Remember, you are not alone. There is a community of people who understand what you have been through and who are ready to support you. Take each day as it comes, and trust in your ability to overcome any challenge. Your new beginning is just around the corner, and I am confident that you will thrive.

With heartfelt encouragement and unwavering support, I wish you all the best on your journey to a brighter, happier future.

References

Emedicine. (n.d.). *Narcissistic personality disorder.*

Mendez, E. (2023, April 12). *17 signs you're married to a narcissist.* Verywell Mind.

Cherney, K. (2023, January 30). *Gaslighting: What it is, long-term effects, and what to do.* Medical News Today.

McLeod, S. (2023, August 15). *Narcissistic abuse cycle: Stages, impact, and coping.* Verywell Mind.

Atlanta Divorce Law Group. (n.d.). *Strategies for divorcing a person with a high-conflict personality.*

The Hotline. (2022, November 8). *Building your case: How to document abuse.*

Ingram, S. (2022, November 30). *What to expect when divorcing a narcissist.*

Thomas, T. (n.d.). *Divorcing a narcissist: Finding the right attorney.* One Mom's Battle.

The Hotline. (n.d.). *Create your personal safety plan.*

McGillin, S. (n.d.). *The importance of documenting everything during a divorce.* MGLS, PC..

National Network to End Domestic Violence. (n.d.). *The impact of safe housing on survivors of domestic violence.*

U.S. Department of Justice. (n.d.). *Federal domestic violence laws.*

Creative Planning. (n.d.). *How to divide your money in a divorce.*

Fidelity Investments. (n.d.). *Tips for budgeting after divorce.*

Mission Wealth. (2023, March 27). *How financial advisors assist before, during, and after a divorce.*

Van Boom, D. (2024, August 1). *Best budgeting apps of August 2024.* Forbes.

Ackerman, C. E. (2023, January 5). *7+ trauma-focused cognitive behavioral therapy exercises and worksheets.* PositivePsychology.com.

Ackerman, C. E. (2023, February 15). *Somatic experiencing therapy: 10 best exercises.* PositivePsychology.com.

Kral, T. R. A., & Davidson, R. J. (2019). *Brief mindfulness meditation improves emotion processing.* Frontiers in Psychology, 10, 592.

Therapy Helpers. (n.d.). *Rebuilding self-esteem after narcissistic abuse..*

Custody X Change. (n.d.). *Co-parenting with a narcissist: Tips and strategies..*

Hall, C. (2018, March 20). *10 strategies for dealing with your narcissistic ex.* **PsychCentral.**

Printed in Dunstable, United Kingdom